FREEMASONRY

WEIGHED IN THE BALANCES AND FOUND WANTING

ELMER N. GARITSON

Lighthouse Publishing Company

P.O. Box 453

Middletown, Ohio 45042

First Printing 1990

Printed in the United States of America

Library of Congress Catalog Card Number: 90-92113
ISBN 0-9628043-0-4

TABLE OF CONTENTS

Dedicated
to
The Glory of God
and
His Cause On Earth

Acknowledgements

Many thanks to my brothers and sisters in the Lord who were aware of this endeavor and prayed for me during the long hours of research and study to make this work for God a reality. Thanks to Fred Boomer who did such a wonderful job on the photography, and to Jim King who supervised the whole project, including printing, photography, color separation and layouts. Special thanks to my wife Jackie, who through the years has been a constant source of help and encouragement in my teaching and preaching the gospel of the kingdom of God.

Introduction

Many volumes have been written and published to the world, pretending to embrace the origin, nature and tendency of free-masonry. Most of the standard works of the institution have identified it with the bible, making its origin from God, its nature divine, and its influence the most favorable on the eternal happiness of the soul. This work is designed to show, that free-masonry is an impostor; that it is founded in error, and is opposed to the Christian religion and to the free institutions of our country.

I come to lay before the world the claims of an institution which has been sanctioned by ages, venerated for wisdom, and exalted for "light"; but, an institution whose benefits have always been overrated, and whose continuance is not, in the slightest degree necessary. We meet it with its high requirements, its "time honored customs", its swelling titles, and shall show it in its nakedness and simplicity.

To some men it is irritating and humiliating in the extreme to give up their darling systems. With the increase of years their fondness becomes so great that they cling to them with wild and bewildered attachment. But we would ask them, where now are the Knights of Malta and Jerusalem, and the objects that called forth their perils and journeying? Where are the crusades and excursions on which our grand Commanders, Generalissimos, and Sir Knights are to be engaged?

The days and occasions that called forth these deeds of chivalry and valor have passed like those of the flood; and the mock dignitaries and puppet-show actions of masons in their imitation call forth pity and indignation. When, we now see the gaudy show in a lodge room, and a train of nominal officers, with their distinctions and badges, it may give us some faint idea of scenes that are past, and may gratify an idle curiosity, but produce no substantial good under heaven.

When monasteries and cloisters, and inquisitor's cells and prisons have been broke up before the sweeping march of the moral mind, why this unnecessary mummery should be so much supported or approved in this country, above all other countries in the world, is amazing to me.

This book is sent forth with the prayer that its message might serve as a help to those people being taken in by the Masonic lodge, and that their eyes might be opened unto the truth of God's word. 2 Cor. 4:4 *"In whom the God of this world blinded the minds of them which believe not, lest the light of the glorious gospel of Christ, who is the image of God, should shine unto them."*

I have many friends who are masons, and I know that this book will cause offense to many, and for that I am sorry. But please keep in mind that what is said is of the Masonic lodge, as an organization, and not of the individual members who may have been more or less deceived.

Millions of souls are being blindly led into the pits of hell because professing Christian ministers, laymen and Sunday School teachers have, either knowingly or ignorantly, joined hands with the DEVIL to deceive the people.

It is not easy for a minister of the gospel to attack that which is held in high esteem by so many people, but the duty of the preacher is very plain in the light of the following scriptures: Isa. 58:1 "*Cry aloud, spare not, lift up thy voice like a trumpet, and show my people their transgression.*" Eph. 5:11 "*Have no fellowship with the unfruitful works of darkness, but rather reprove them.*" 1 John 1:16 "*If we say that we have fellowship with him, and walk in darkness, we lie, and do not the truth.*"

One of the greatest needs in the church today, is for preachers to cry out against the idolatrous evils of the Masonic lodge. Freemasonry clothes its pagan doctrines in the garb of Christian truth with the hope that it will not be exposed. It is hard to reach error when it hides under truth, but in this respect it is no different than any other cult that we must deal with in this present world.

A mason cannot become a Christian without violating his Masonic obligation, and a Christian cannot become a mason without violating his Christian obligation. Brethren! masonry cannot live in the church of God. This is not its element —it belongs to the world. There must ultimately be a separation. Almighty God solemnly reminds us all, that "He will bring every work into judgement, with every secret thing, In the day when God shall judge the secrets of men by Jesus Christ."

Elmer N. Garitson, Minister
First Church of God

Structure of Freemasonry

THE TO ALL

TRUE AND FAITHFUL MEMBERS, GREETING!

KNOW YE THAT OUR WORTHY BROTHER

____

WAS REGULARLY RECEIVED, ADMITTED AND CREATED A

NOBLE OF THE MYSTIC SHRINE,

In __________ *Temple, at* ______________

On the __________ *day of* __________ *A.D. 19* ______

AND THAT HE HAS BEEN DULY ENROLLED AS SUCH UPON THE

RECORDS OF THE ORDER.

In Testimony Whereof, We, the

ILLUSTRIOUS POTENTATE AND ILL. RECORDER,

Have hereunto subscribed our names and affixed The Seal of The Temple

AT ITS OASIS IN THE

City of ______________ *State of* ______________

ATTEST:

ILLUSTRIOUS RECORDER

ILLUSTRIOUS POTENTATE

Certificate of Initiation

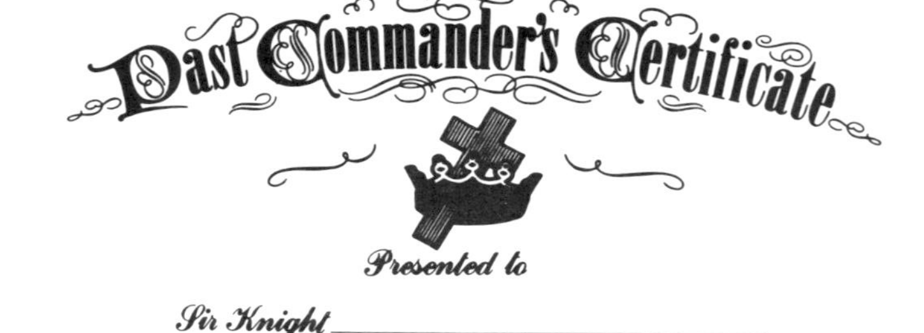

Past Commander's Certificate

Presented to

Sir Knight ______________________

In Recognition of his Distinguished Service to Templary and to

Commandery No. , Knights Templar,

, State of ,

While Serving as Eminent Commander for the Year 19___.

Presented this ____ Day of __________ 19___

By

______________________ Commander

______________________ Generalissimo

______________________ Captain General

Attest ______________________ Recorder

Macoy Publishing & Masonic Supply Co., Inc., Richmond, VA

Chapter 1

MASONRY IS A RELIGION

It is often said, that masonry is nothing more than a civil institution, designed to promote a knowledge of the arts and sciences; and to improve the conditions of human life; that it has no connection with religion, and no concern with the salvation of men. This is not true.

Is masonry not a religion simply because it does not identify itself as a religion? I am going to quote from an article out of my notebook on the Masonic lodge. I cut this out of a booklet on masonry and failed to write down the author's name: "Christian science, via Mary Baker Eddy, teaches that when a man's heart stops beating and he dies, it is not really death, but only an illusion. Christian Science boldly claims there is no such thing as pain, evil, sickness, or death; there is only good. But if there is only good where do the illusions of evil come from? Most people realize that calling death something different (an illusion) does not change what it really is.

The same is true of masonry. Masonry does not call itself a religion. But most people realize that identifying itself as a fraternal organization instead of a religion does not change what it really is in practice.

Alva J. McClain, in his book, **Freemasonry and Christianity** says: "The man who contends that Freemasonry is not a religious institution is childishly ignorant of the organization or else he is a willful deceiver. Masonry is religious - it teaches religion."

Daniel Sickles 33°, in the **Ahiman Rezon** (pp. 7-8) says: "Masonry teaches the most sublime truths and points out to its disciples a correct knowledge of the Great Architect of the Universe, and the moral laws he has ordained for their government."

Evidently, that institution whose main object is to teach Divine Truth - the truth of God and of the soul - the nature and essence of both; whose practical purpose is to fashion the morality of man in accordance with such theory, is a religion.

Also A.T.C. Pierson, another well known Masonic author, in his book, the **Traditions of Freemasonry** (p. 13) says: "The order known as Freemasonry appears to have been instituted as a vehicle to preserve and transmit an account of the miraculous dealings of the Most High with his people in the infancy of the world, for at that early period Freemasonry may be identified with religion."

Despite the evidence that masonry displays all the characteristics of a religion, many masons will deny the obvious and insist that the lodge is religious but not a religion.

Henry W. Coil 33°, in Coil's Encyclopedia, Art. Religion, says: "some attempt to avoid the issue by saying that Freemasonry is not a religion but is religious, seeming to believe that the substitution of an adjective for a noun makes a fundamental difference. It would be as sensible to say that a man had no intellect but was intellectual or that he had no honor but was honorable. Freemasonry certainly requires a belief in the existence of, and man's dependence upon, a Supreme Being to which he is responsible. What can a church add to that, except to bring into fellowship those who have like feelings? That is exactly what the lodge does. It is said that Freemasonry is not sectarian, by which is meant that it has not identified itself with any well-known sect. But, if it has a religious credo, may it not, itself, constitute a sect to be added to the others? Perhaps the most we can say is that Freemasonry has not generally been regarded as a sect or denomination, though it may become so if its religious practices, creeds, tenets, and dogma increase as much in the future as they have in the past. Only by judging from external appearances and applying arbitrary gauges can we say that Freemasonry is not a religion. The difference between a lodge and a church is one of degree and not of kind. For example, the lodge is not as highly organized in its ceremony as the Roman Catholic Church, but it is actually more organized than a church of Friends (Quakers)." Coil reminds masons that "The fact that Freemasonry is a MILD religion does nor mean that it is NO religion."

Again in the Encyclopedia (p. 512) Coil says: "The oft repeated aphorism: Freemasonry is not a religion, but is most emphatically religion's handmaid, has been challenged as meaningless, which it seems to be. Does Freemasonry continually teach and insist upon a creed, tenet, and dogma? Does it have meetings characterized by the practice of rites and ceremonies in and by which its creed, tenet, and dogma are illustrated by myths, symbols, and allegories? If Freemasonry were not a religion, what would have to be done to make it such? Nothing would be necessary or at least nothing but to add more of the same."

J.S.M. Ward 33°, in **Freemasonry: Its Aims and Ideals** (p.71) says: "I am aware that many masons object strongly to the idea that Freemasonry is religious. Yet if there is anything in the contention of those who hold that in Freemasonry we may trace mystical teachings as to the nature of God, clearly masonry is religious, even if some hesitate to call it a religion.

In fact the controversy is due entirely to the use of loose terminology. Freemasonry is not a dogmatic faith, but it teaches certain fundamental religious truths such as, what is the nature of God, and that after death men live. These are distinct tenets, and no amount of beating around the bush can disguise the fact. Further, I go so far as to contend that the main object of Freemasonry is to teach the mystical life and union with the Divine."

Again, Ward states in the same book, (pp.184-185) "Freemasonry teaches definitely that there is a God, in the main similar to the Jewish conception of Jehovah, but, according to the Royal Arch, of a triune nature quite unknown to the old Testament, viz., Creative, Preservative, and Annihilative: in short, similar to Trimurti of the Hindoos, who unites in One Person the Creative aspect of Brahma, the Preservative attributes of Vishnu, and the Destructive character of Shiva. I consider Freemasonry is a sufficiently organized school of mysticism to be entitled to be called a religion."

Albert C. Mackey 33°, in his **Encyclopedia of Freemasonry** (pp. 618-619) states: "On the contrary, I contend without any sort of hesitation, that masonry is, in every sense of the word, an eminently religious institution - that it is indebted solely to the religious element which it contains for its origin and for its continued existence, and that without this religious element it would scarcely be worthy of cultivation by the wise and good.

Look at its ancient landmarks, its sublime ceremonies, its profound symbols and allegories - all inculcating religious doctrine, commanding religious observance, and teaching religious truth, and who can deny that it is eminently a religious institution? Masonry, then, is, indeed a religious institution; and on this ground mainly, if not alone, should the religious mason defend it."

Thomas Webb, in **Webb's Monitor** (p. 284) says: "The meeting of a Masonic lodge is strictly a RELIGIOUS CEREMONY. The religious tenets of Masonry are few and simple, but fundamental."

Albert G. Mackey 33°, in his **Manual of the Lodge**, (p. 46) says: "As masons we are taught never to begin any great or important undertaking without first invoking the blessing and protection of deity, AND THIS IS BECAUSE MASONRY IS A RELIGIOUS INSTITUTION."

Albert Pike 33°, in **Morals and Dogma** (p. 213), says: "Every Masonic Lodge is a temple of religion; and its teachings are instructions in religion."

Albert G. Mackey in his **Lexicon of Freemasonry** (pp. 408-409) says: "Freemasonry does not profess to interfere with the religious opinions of its members. It asks only for a declaration of that simple and universal faith, in which men of all nations and all sects agree, - the belief in a God and in his superintending providence. Beyond this it does not venture, but leaves the minds of its disciples, on other and sectarian points, perfectly untrammeled. This is the only religious qualification required of a candidate, but this is most strictly demanded. THE RELIGION THEN, OF MASONRY, IS PURE THEISM, on which its different members engraft their own peculiar opinions; but they are not permitted to introduce them into the lodge, or to connect their truth or falsehood with the truth of masonry.

Let a man's religion, or mode of worship, be what it may, he is not excluded from the order, provided he believes in the glorious Architect of heaven and earth, and practices the sacred duties of morality. Masons unite with the virtuous of every persuasion, in the firm and pleasing bond of fraternal love; they are taught to view the errors of mankind with compassion, and to strive, by the purity of their own conduct, to demonstrate the superior excellence of the faith they may possess."

J.S.M. Ward in **Freemasonry: Its Aims and Ideals**, (pp. 186-188) states: "Freemasonry nowhere denies any fundamental doctrine of any religion, and in consequence experience has shown that a Christian, a Jew, a Hindoo, and a Mohammedan can all be masons, and yet remain loyal to their faiths. If there was any real conflict between masonry and any religion, assuredly it would have arisen with one of these diverse types. In reality, Freemasonry teaches those spiritual truths on which all religions are based and which are common to all, and leaves its sons to add such further embellishments as they themselves consider true and desirable."

Now it is plain that "that religion in which all men agree," and that which is acceptable to the Jew, Buddhist, Mohammedan, Hindoo, "and the worshipper of Deity under every form," is essentially and necessarily anti-christian. In none of the religions just mentioned do all men agree! Therefore, the religion of Masonry must be a religion entirely peculiar to itself.

Let us continue. Mr. Ward says, "No religion is endangered by Freemasonry; but, on the other hand, there is no room for bigots in our order. Each man is entitled to think his conception of the truth is the best, but he is not entitled to interfere with the conception of the Truth held by another. The aim of Freemasonry is to combat Atheism and gross Materialism, to set men's feet on the path of salvation and to help them towards the Light; but it holds that there be many paths that lead to the throne of the All-Loving Father which all start from a common source. Freemasonry believes that though these paths appear to branch off in various directions, yet they all reach the same ultimate goal, and that to some men one path is better and to others another; and so with tender tolerance and real Christian charity it bids all its children God-speed on the Mystic Quest, which ends in union with the same God whether we call Him Jehovah, Allah, Trimurti, or just "Our Father which art in heaven." No truly religious man need fear to enter Freemasonry, or imagine that to belong to our Order will in any way undermine his present faith; rather it will confirm his belief in the Fatherhood of God when he sees, as I have done, men of every race and creed unite in the same prayers in Lodge.

Thus, in answer to this question, I boldly declare that Freemasonry IS A RELIGION, yet in no way conflicts with any other religion, unless that religion holds that no one outside its portals can be saved. But if there is any man contemplating joining our Order who really believes that the All-Loving Father has consigned to everlasting hell the majority of the human race, just because they do not see eye to eye with him in religious matters, then assuredly he should not join Freemasonry, for he is not a fit and proper person to be made a Mason."

From all of the above testimonies, furnished by Masonic text-books and written by their most honored teachers and authors, what are we to believe but that Masonry is a RELIGIOUS institution and that its teachings are instructions in religion.

MASONRY CLAIMS TO BE A UNIVERSAL RELIGION

Not only does Freemasonry see itself as a religion, but it sees itself as the universal religion, while Christianity is simply another sect whose particular beliefs have divided mankind over the ages. It pretends to select the best features of Christianity, Mohammedanism, Hinduism, Buddhism, Confucianism, etc. It attempts to become a common denominator for all the world religions, in which men of every faith may join on an equal plane.

Manly P. Hall 33°, in **The Lost Keys of Freemasonry** (p. 65) says: "The true Mason is not creed-bound. He realizes with the divine illumination of his lodge that as a Mason his religion must be universal: Christ, Buddha or Mohammed, the name means little, for he recognizes only the light and not the bearer. He worships at every shrine, bows before every altar, whether in temple, mosque or cathedral, realizing with his truer understanding the oneness of all spiritual truth."

Joseph Fort Newton, Litt. D., Grand Lodge of Iowa, in **The Men's House**, (p. 156) says: "The saying of Penn is a perfect statement of the historic attitude of Masonry: "All just men, all devout men, are everywhere of one religion, and when death hath taken off the masks they will know one another." But why wait for death to remove the masks? Masonry teaches no religion save that religion of all good men which underlies all sects and out-tops all creeds."

H.L. Haywood, Masonic author, in his book entitled **The Great Teachings of Masonry**, (p. 115) says: "William Penn believed that death would remove our masks and that we would all then discover ourselves to be of one religion. The Universality of Freemasonry lifts the masks of all differences now and proves that we are all united in our humanity, that God has made of one blood all nations that dwell upon the face of the earth.

Freemasonry makes no attempts to adjudicate the religious quarrels of the race. It does not take the position that there is one true religion among a great many religions wholly false. Its position is entirely its own. It takes the position that, letting religions be as they are, they one and all possess certain fundamentals everywhere alike, and it is on these fundamentals that Masonry takes its stand."

Thomas Webb, a Masonic author, in **Webb's Monitor**, (p. 285) states: "So broad is the religion of Masonry, and so CAREFULLY ARE ALL SECTARIAN TENETS EXCLUDED FROM THE SYSTEM, that the Christian, the Jew, and the

Mohammedan, in all of their numberless sects and divisions, may, and do harmoniously combine in the moral and intellectual work with the Buddhist, the Parsee, the Confucian, and the worshipper of Deity under every form."

Albert Pike 33°, and one of the most important American authorities, in **Morals and Dogma**, (p. 226) says: "Masonry, around whose altars the Christian, the Hebrew, the Moslem, the Brahmin, the followers of Confucius and Zoroaster, can assemble as brethren and unite in prayer to the one God who is above ALL the Baalim, must needs leave it to each of its initiates to look for the foundation of his faith and hope to the written scriptures of his own religion."

The word, Baalim, according to Unger's Bible Dictionary, is simply defined as "false gods". Albert Pike has included the God of the Christians in that category. So by this statement we can see that the God of the bible is not the God that masons pray to.

Again Albert Pike in **Morals and Dogma**, (p. 524) states: "we do not undervalue the importance of any Truth. We utter no word that can be deemed irreverent by any one of any faith. We do not tell the Moslem that it is only important for him to believe that there is but one God, and wholly unessential whether Mahomet was his prophet. We do not tell the Hebrew that the Messiah whom he expects was born in Bethlehem nearly two thousand years ago and that he is a heretic because he will not so believe. And as little do we tell the sincere Christian that Jesus of Nazareth was but a man like us, or His history but the unreal revival of an older legend. To do either is beyond our jurisdiction. Masonry, of no one age, belongs to all time; of no one religion, it finds its great truths in all.

To every Mason, there is a God. How, or by what intermediates He creates and acts, and in what way He unfolds and manifests Himself, Masonry leaves to creeds and Religions to inquire."

J.D. Buck, M.D., another Masonic writer of importance, in his book, **Mystic Masonry** (pp. 46-47) wrote: "The candidate is taught, not merely to tolerate another's religion, but to respect it as his own; though still adhering to that in which he was born. To make reasonable this obligation, he is shown through the Kabalah or Secret Doctrine that, at the heart of every great religion, lie the same eternal truths. Forms and observances only differ. Masonry is not only a universal science, but a world-wide religion, and owes allegiance to no one creed, and can adopt no sectarian dogma, as such, without ceasing thereby to be Masonic. Drawn from the Kabalah, and taking the Jewish or Christian verbiage or symbols, it but discerns in them universal truths, which it recognizes in all other religions. Many degrees have been Christianized only to perish; as every degree eventually will if circumscribed by narrow creeds, and dwarfed to the bigoted apprehension, so as to exclude good men of any other communion. Masonry is the Universal Religion only because, and only so long, as it embraces all religions. For this reason, and this alone, it is universal and eternal."

Albert Mackey 33°, in **The Encyclopedia of Freemasonry**, Art.- Religion of Masonry, says: "The religion of Masonry is not sectarian. It admits men of every creed within its hospitable bosom, rejecting none and approving none for his peculiar faith. It is not Judaism, though there is nothing in it to offend a Jew: it is not Christianity, but there is nothing in it repugnant to the faith of a Christian. Its religion is that general one of nature and primitive revelation - handed down to us from some ancient and patriarchal priesthood - in which all men may agree and in which no man can differ."

Albert Mackey, 33°, in the same Encyclopedia (p. 149) says: "If Masonry were simply a Christian institution, the Jew and the Moslem, the Brahman and the Buddhist, could not conscientiously partake of its illumination. But its universality is its boast. In its language citizens of every nation may converse; at its altar men of all religions may kneel; to its creed disciples of every faith may subscribe."

Albert Pike, 33° in **Morals and Dogma**, (p. 38) states: "Catholicism was a vital truth in its earliest ages, but it became obsolete, and Protestantism arose, flourished, and deteriorated. The doctrines of Zoroaster were the best which the ancient Persians were fitted to receive; those of Confucius were fitted for the Chinese; those of Mohammed for the idolatrous Arabs of his age. Each was Truth for the time. Each was a Gospel, preached by a Reformer; and if any men are so little fortunate as to remain content therewith, when others have attained a higher truth, it is their misfortune and not their fault. They are to be pitied for it, and not persecuted."

As therefore, all these ancient religions, Christianity included, are only "Truth for the time," the best that a race or country, according to its degree of barbarism or imperfect enlightenment, is fitted to receive. The Christian soul which is not satisfied with this must be squeamish indeed. But if this is not enough, Masonry will widen the bounds of its tolerance, as we have seen, and pity those who, having a nobler faith proposed to them, the pure faith of the Kabalah, are still content to grope their way in the darkness of obsolete Christianity.

Alphonse Cerza, 33° in his book entitled **Let There Be Light** (p.43) quotes M.W. Thomas S. Roy, D.D., now Past Grand Master of the Grand Lodge of Massachusetts saying: "When Freemasonry accepts a Christian, or a Jew, or a Buddhist, or a Mohammedan, it does not accept him as such, but as a man, worthy to be received into the Order. It is the glory of Masonry that a man who believes implicitly in the deity of Christ, and a man who says he cannot go that far, can meet as BROTHERS in their acknowledgment of the sovereignty of the supreme Being, the Maker of Heaven and earth, and in acknowledgment of their duty to love Him with heart and mind and soul and strength."

The above statement, is just one of many, that shows Masonic ignorance when it comes to the Word of God. The Bible lies on a Masonic Altar, like it lies on a coffee table, in a lot of homes - it is mostly for show. 2 Cor. 6:14 - *"Be ye not unequally yoked together with unbelievers."* In the light of this scripture alone, tell me how a man who believes implicitly in the deity of Christ, and a man who says he cannot go that far, can possibly meet as BROTHERS! I John 2:22 - *"Who is a liar but he that denieth that Jesus is the Christ?"* and John 3:36 - *"He that believeth on the son hath everlasting life: and he that believeth not the Son shall not see life; but the wrath of God abideth on him."*

No Christian can stand on the platform of universality. The moment he admits the equality of other religions with Christianity, he has denied the fundamental doctrine of his faith. In 1 Cor. 3:11 we read - *"For other foundation can no man lay than that is laid, which is Jesus Christ."* When a minister joins the lodge and becomes a mason, he is saying, in so many words, that one foundation is as good as another, one religion is as good as another.

Masonry is not only a universal religion, but it is also a paganistic religion which includes Sun-Worship. For additional information on this subject see chapter 4, Hiram Abiff.

SUN WORSHIP

Albert Mackey 33°, in **Symbolism of Freemasonry**, (pp. 28, 34) "Many, indeed nearly all, of the Masonic symbols of the present day can only be thoroughly comprehended and properly appreciated by this reference to sun worship....the religious system of Masonry comes from the East, and has reference to the primitive religion, whose first occupation was the worship of the sun."

Albert Pike 33°, in **Morals and Dogma**, (p. 476) says: "The sun was termed by the Greeks the Eye of Jupiter, and the Eye of the world; and his is the all-seeing Eye in our lodges."

Carl Claudy, a well known Masonic writer, says in **Introduction to Freemasonry** (p.31) "The sun seems to move from east to west by way of the south. Early man circled altars, on which burned the fire which was his God, from east to west by way of the south. Circumambulation became a part of all religious observances; it was in the ceremonies of ancient Egypt; it was part of the mysteries of Eleusis; it was practiced in the rites of Mithras and a thousand other cults, and down through the ages it has come to us."

Carl Claudy, in same book listed above, (p. 107) says: "The sun is the Past Master's own symbol; our Masters rule their lodges - or are supposed to! - with the same regularity with which the sun rules the day and the moon governs the night. In circumambulation about the altar we traverse our lodges from East to West by way of the South as did the sun worshipers who thus imitated the daily passage of their diety through the heavens."

Rollin C. Blackmer, Past Master, Past High Priest, Past commander, in his book entitled, **The Lodge and the Craft**, (p. 172) gives the following prayer at the grave: "O Sun and all the Gods that give light to men, and Thou Great God who art above all gods and of whom all other Gods are but names and attributes, Eternal God of nature and revelation! Thou who in Thy world of nature doth raise tree and grass and flower from the death of winter to the life of spring!....."

Albert Mackey in **Manual of the Lodge** (p. 24) says: "The circumambulation among the pagan nations referred to the great doctrine of Sabaism, or sun-worship. Freemasonry alone has preserved the primitive meaning, which was a symbolic allusion to the sun, as the source of physical light and the most wonderful work of the 'Grand Architect of the Universe.' The lodge represents the world; the three principal officers represents the sun in her three principal positions - at rising, at meridian, and at setting.

This proves beyond a doubt, that Masonry is the religious philosophy of Baal, revived, and that the Sun-god is constantly referred to in all the other ceremonies of initiation,

A.T.C. Pierson in **Traditions of Freemasonry**, (pp. 87-88) states: "It is evident then that the sun either as an object of worship or of symbolization has always formed an important part of both the 'Mysteries' and the system of Freemasonry."

No matter which way you turn in Masonry, or what emblem you investigate, you cannot get outside of the influence of Sun-Worship. Look at the Past Master's apron, ring, etc., etc.

Chapter 2

WORKING TOOLS OF MASONRY

Christianity teaches the doctrines and precepts of morality in plain language, and in a plain, simple manner; but masonry pretends to teach them by emblems and ceremonies.

The law of ceremonies which was anciently instituted by God, has been abolished; and no person or persons are at liberty to revive it or introduce another. Many of the Masonic ceremonies are well known to be ancient Jewish ceremonies. These have long since fulfilled the purposes for which they were instituted, have been blotted out and nailed to the cross by our loving Saviour. What authority have masons for reviving them? They have none. They are insulting Almighty God; and contending with him, that his Son has not fulfilled the law and the prophets, nor become the end of the law for righteousness; but was an impostor, and all it is said he has done, is a lie.

These ceremonies, as instituted by God, had some meaning; they were a shadow of good things to come, and exhibited in a lively figure the whole gospel dispensation. But this meaning masons have perverted. Their ceremonies do not have the morality of Jesus Christ in them, and are not a shadow of good things to come.

They may tell us that certain things in their institution are designed to teach certain truths, and to be emblems of certain virtues; but by whose authority, and what instruction can they give us from these things? Where has the Lord informed us, in his word, that a chisel, a mallet, a square, a compass, a trowel, a scythe, and a white leather apron, are emblems of the virtues of the human heart, and are designed to inculcate moral truths? Masonry tells us that a habitual practice of every commendable virtue, is taught by suitable and appropriate Masonic emblems. Now God has taught us these things in his word, in plain and definite language; but not by chisels, and mallets, and white leather aprons, and other Masonic symbols. I may just as well say, that the set of balances that I am using on the cover of this book, are emblems of the virtues of the heart, and are designed to teach moral truths. I would be as nobly employed, should I attempt to communicate religious instruction from these, to lost dying men, as from a chisel or a mallet. My authority is as good in one case as in the other.

Albert G. Mackey 33° in his book **Lexicon of Freemasonry** (p. 163) states concerning the gavel: "The common gavel is one of the working tools of an Entered Apprentice. It is made use of by the Operative Mason to break off the corners of the rough ashlar, and thus fit it the better for the builder's use, and is therefore adopted as a symbol in Speculative Masonry to admonish us of the duty of divesting our minds and consciences of all the vices and impurities of life, thereby fitting our bodies as living stones for that spiritual building not made with hands, eternal in the heavens."

James L. Gould 33° Past Grand High Priest, in his book entitled **Guide To Royal Arch Masonry** (p. 167) we read: "The working tools of a royal arch mason are the crow, pickax, and spade. The crow is used by operative masons to raise things of great weight and bulk; the pickax to loosen the soil, and prepare it for digging; and the spade to remove rubbish. But the royal arch mason is emblematically taught to use them for more noble purposes. By them he is reminded that it is his sacred duty to lift from his mind the heavy weight of passions and prejudices which encumber his progress toward virtue, loosening the hold which long habits of sin and folly have had upon his disposition, and removing the rubbish of vice and ignorance, which prevents him from beholding that eternal foundation of truth and wisdom upon which he is to erect the spiritual and moral temple of his second life."

What need is there of all this? Is not the duty of man plainly taught him in the bible? He who leaves this precious word and goes to Masonic emblems for moral instruction, is like one who leaves a pure fountain for a filthy puddle. All the religious information fallen man needs, God has communicated in his written word, and in a manner so very plain and simple, that the lowest human capacity may understand it with no other teacher than the Holy Spirit. 2 Peter 1:3 - *"According as his divine power hath given unto us all things that pertain unto life and godliness, through the knowledge of him that hath called us to glory and virtue."*

Daniel Sickels 33°, in his book entitled **The General Ahiman Rezon** (p. 65) states: "The three great Lights in Masonry are the Holy Bible, Square, and Compasses, and are thus explained:

The Holy Bible is given us as a rule and guide of our faith and practice; the Square, to square our actions; and the Compasses to circumscribe our desires, and keep our passions in due bounds with all mankind, especially with the brethren."

As far as I'm concerned, Masonry could get by with just one great Light - the Bible. If we live by it, as we should, we wouldn't have to worry about squaring our actions or letting our desires and passions get out of control.

In Vol. 2 of **Scottish Rite Masonry**, (p. 212) 28th Degree, Knights of the Sun, we read: "His body being relieved from ignominy, his mind may now discover and fulfill the moral meaning of the cone or pyramid; that form of matter from which all other figures may be derived, and which is an emblem of productive truth, varied order and economic utility. It represents the true mason who RAISES HIMSELF by degrees till he reaches heaven, to adore the sacred and unutterable name of the Great Architect of the Universe. "- - - - - - "The soul that is impure and sinful and defiled with earthly stains cannot again unite with God, until by LONG TRIALS AND MANY PURIFICATIONS it is finally delivered from the old calamity, and light overcomes darkness and dethrones it in the soul." Reader, can you not see how masonry is trying to replace salvation by grace with that of human works.

In Vol. 1 of **Scottish Rite Masonry**, (p. 450) 17th Degree, Knights of the East and West, we read:

Senior Warden - "They are those who came here after passing through great tribulation and having washed their robes in THEIR OWN BLOOD. Will you purchase such robes at so great a price?"

Candidate - "Yes; I am willing": Wardens then conduct him to the basin, bare his arms, tie a string or bandage around each arm, when each with a lancet makes a trifling incision so as barely to draw blood which is wiped on a napkin and exhibited.

Senior Warden - "See my brethren a man who has spilled his blood to acquire a knowledge of our mysteries and shrunk not from the trial!"

In Vol. 2 of **Scottish Rite Masonry**, (p. 209) 28th Degree Initiation, Knights of the Sun, we read:

Father Adam - What more does thou desire?

Brother Truth - (For candidate) To DIVEST MYSELF of original sin and renounce the juvenile prejudices of error which all men are liable to; namely the desire of all worldly attachments and pride,

In the above paragraphs we can readily see how masonry teaches its candidates salvation by works, rather than salvation by grace through the shed blood of Jesus. And yet, the worshipful Master has the nerve to say to the candidate upon initiation, that there is nothing in this obligation that will conflict with your religion. Masonry teaches the candidate that he can DIVEST HIMSELF of original sin, MAKE HIMSELF deserving of entering heaven, and also that his soul can be united with GOD by LONG TRIALS AND MANY PURIFICATIONS. These are doctrines of Devils, and the Masonic Lodge is the Synagogue of Satan.

We are informed by Masonry, that the apostasy of man is exhibited in a lively manner by Masonic representations. "In view of this state, naked and exposed to the Divine displeasure, the candidate is constrained to look forward to the great source and fountain whence all his temporal as well as spiritual wants may be supplied." Must a man, to learn that he is a fallen creature, go to a Masonic lodge, and there pass through some kind of ceremony, which shall exhibit in action the naked, exposed, and wretched condition of Adam; and be told that this represents his apostasy, and that he is exposed to the Divine displeasure? Is there no other way in which he may be taught this? Let him read in God's word, *"by one man sin entered into the world, and death by sin, and so death passed upon all men, for that all have sinned."* Rom. 5:12. This will teach him without any kind of ceremony, that he is a sinner, and is exposed to Divine displeasure. It may carry conviction to his heart, and such conviction as shall terminate in his repentance, reformation, and return to God. What conviction did these Masonic ceremonies ever have on the heart of a sinful being? Tell us of the true repentance, the brokenness and contrition of heart produced by them.

We are further told, that there are many things in a Masonic lodge, which represents the doctrine of the Trinity. Masonry says, "The lodge is emblematically supported by three grand pillars - the principal officers are three - three articles constitute the furniture; the Holy bible, the square, and the compass;" and many other things they mention of a similar nature. It would be gratifying if the lodge would show us their authority, if they have any, for telling people that these things represent the doctrine of the Trinity. Does not Masonry know, and does not every one who is educated in the Christian religion know, that there is no representation or likeness of this awful mystery? The person or organization who makes such a representation is not far from idolatry!

The superstitious Hindoos made a god with three faces to represent the same idea. There is as much of the Christian religion in this heathen figure, as in three grand pillars, or any other Masonic representation. Who is guilty of the greatest folly and superstition, and even wickedness, ignorant Hindoos, or enlightened masons? Is it true that three grand pillars, or three officers, or three articles of furniture, the holy bible, the square and compass, are emblematical of the adorable Three, who bare record in heaven, and are one? How strange that men of professed piety should pretend such things! If a person wishes to learn more of God, of himself, and duty, let him go to the bible, that sure word of prophecy, and not to Masonic emblems.

Chapter 3

THE LAMB SKIN APRON

It is not ornamental, the cost is not great,
 There are other things far more useful, yet truly I state,
Tho of all my possessions, there's none can compare,
 With that white leather apron, which all Masons wear.

As a young lad I wondered just what it all meant,
 When dad hustled around, and so much time was spent,
On shaving and dressing and looking just right,
 Until mother would say: "Its the Masons tonight."

And some winter nights she said: "What makes you go,
 Way up there tonight thru the sleet and the snow,
You see the same things every month of the year,
 Then dad would reply: "Yes, I know it, my dear,

Forty years I have seen the same things, it is true,
 And though they are old, they always seem new,
For the hands that I clasp, and the friends that I greet,
 Seem a little bit closer each time that we meet."

Years later I stood at that very same door,
 With good men and true who had entered before,
I knelt at the altar, and there I was taught
 That virtue and honor can never be bought.

That the spotless white lambskin all Masons revere,
 If worthily worn grows more precious each year,
That service to others brings blessings untold,
 That man may be poor tho surrounded by gold.

I learned that true brotherhood flourishes there,
 That enmities fade neath the compass and square,
That wealth and position are all thrust aside,
 As there on the level men meet and abide.

So, Honor the lambskin, may it always remain
Forever unblemished, and free from all stain,
And when we are called to the Great Father's love,
May we all take our place in that Lodge up above.

Daniel Sickels in **The Ahiman Rezon** (p. 67) makes the following statement: "After the candidate has been initiated into the first degree and has become pure and innocent, he is given the white lambskin apron, which "is his badge as a mason, a sign of his purification and innocence." It is to be laid upon his coffin and buried with him, and ENTITLES him to eternal reward."

A.T.C. Pierson in his book **Traditions Of Freemasonry** (pp. 44-45) says: "There is no one of the symbols of masonry more important in its teachings, or more interesting in its history, than that of the lambskin or white leather apron. When a candidate was initiated into the ancient mysteries, he was esteemed regenerate, and he was invested with a white garment and apron as a symbol of his newly attained purity."

W. L. Wilmhurst, a Past Master, in his book **The Meaning Of Masonry** (p. 37) has this to say concerning the apron and gloves: "who" says the Psalmist (and remember that the Psalms were the sacred hymns used in the Hebrew mysteries), "Who will go up to the hill of the Lord, and ascend to his holy place? Even he that hath clean hands and a pure heart;" whence it comes that we wear white gloves and aprons as emblems that WE have purified our hearts and washed our hands in innocency." Reader, you can wear all the white accessories you want, but if you haven't been born-again and had the blood of Jesus Christ applied to your heart and soul by faith, you are still unclean and guilty before God. Pilate washed his hands also - but they weren't clean - He was still a sinner!

W. L. Wilmhurst, a little further on in the same book (p. 39) says: "Happy then is the mason who has so far purified and developed HIS OWN NATURE as to realize in its fullness the meaning of the "sacred symbol" of the second degree, and found God present not outside but within himself. By perfecting his conduct, by struggles against his own natural propensities, the candidate is working the rough ashlar of his own nature into the perfect cube. [In other words he is perfecting his own salvation]

The inward development which the second degree symbolizes is typified by the lowering of the triangular flap of the apron upon the rectangular portion below. This is equivalent to the rite of confirmation in the Christian church. It denotes "the progress we have made in the science", or in other words it indicates that the higher nature of the man, symbolized by the Trinity of spirit, has descended into and is now permeating his lower nature."

Again Wilmhurst in **The Meaning of Masonry** (p. 136) states that: "The unadorned white apron of the first degree indicates the purity of soul contemplated as being attained in that degree. The pale blue rosettes added to the apron in the second degree indicate that progress is being made in the science of regeneration and that the candidate's spirituality is beginning to develop and bud through. Blue, the colour of the sky, is traditionally associated with devotion to spiritual concerns. In the third degree still further progress is emblematized by the increased blue adornments of the apron, as also by its silver tassels and the silver serpent used to fasten the apron-strings. The silver serpent is the emblem of Divine Wisdom knitting the soul's new-made vesture together.

In John 3:3 Jesus never told Nicodemus that the new-birth was a "science" which he attained by degrees, nor did he invest him with a white leather apron as a token of innocence.

George Steinmetz in **Freemasonry: Its Hidden Meaning** (p. 65) says: "The flap of an apron turned up appears as a triangle surmounting a square. In this position it symbolizes the "two" men separated. The square below is the material man with no spiritual part. The triangle above represents the spiritual, hovering over, but not yet having entered the material. In evolution it depicts the "brute-man" before the advent of the spiritual, which we term the dawn of conscience."

Again, Steinmetz in the same book (pp. 106-107) says: "When the flap of the apron is turned down, it should appear as a triangle within a square. This symbolizes the spiritual within the material. Hereby man begins the evolution which will eventually end in his assuming the likeness of his Creator."

Of course Mr. Steinmetz doesn't tell us how long this evolutionary process will take before we start assuming the likeness of our Creator. In this respect, it reminds me a lot of the doctrine of Purgatory, where we ask ourselves the question, "how long do we pray and how much do we pay, before our loved ones are released"- Your guess is as good as mine!

Henry W. Coil, 33° in **Coils Masonic Encyclopedia** (pp. 72-73) says: "There is no one of the symbols of Speculative Masonry more important in its teachings, or more interesting in its history, than the lambskin, or white leather apron. Commencing its lessons at an early period in the mason's progress, it is impressed upon his memory as the first gift which he receives, the first symbol which is explained to him, and the first tangible evidence which he possesses of his admission into the Fraternity. Whatever may be his future advancement in the royal art, into whatever deeper arcana his devotion to the mystic institution or his thirst for knowledge may subsequently lead him, with the lambskin apron - his first investure - he never parts. Changing, perhaps, its form and its decorations, and conveying, at each step, some new but still beautiful allusion, its substance is still there, and it continues to claim the honored title by which it was first made known to him, on the night of his initiation, as **the badge of a mason**".

In the Masonic apron two things are essential to the due preservation of its symbolic character - its color and its material.

1- **As to its color**- The color of a mason's apron should be pure unspotted white. This color has, in all ages and countries, been esteemed an emblem of innocence and purity.

2- **As to its material** - A mason's apron must be made of lambskin. The lamb has always been considered as an appropriate emblem of innocence. And hence we are taught, in the ritual of the first degree, that, "by the lambskin", the mason is reminded of that purity of life and rectitude of conduct which is so essentially necessary to his gaining admission into the celestial Lodge above, where the Supreme Architect of the Universe forever presides".

Albert G. Mackey in his **Lexicon of Freemasonry** - Art. Apron (pp. 40-41) says: "By the whiteness of its colour, and the innocence of the animal from which it is obtained, we are admonished to preserve that blameless purity of life and conduct, which will alone enable us hereafter to present ourselves before the Grand Master of the Universe, unstained with sin and unsullied with vice.

Investure constituted an important part of the ancient mysteries; and as the white apron is the investure of masonry, we find something resembling it in all the pagan rites."

Charles T. Powner Co. in their book entitled **Freemasonry Illustrated** (p. 124), note 68, quoting Morris's Dictionary says: "The apron suggests the preservation of the garments from the defilements of labor, and morally the guard of the soul from the defilements of sin. It is therefore the distinguishing badge of a society whose great aim is to prepare the soul for that spiritual building, that house not made with hands, eternal in the heavens."

I want you to look at that last sentence again. "It is therefore the distinguishing badge of a society whose great aim is to prepare the soul...." Now it appears to me, if I am not totally blind, that the Masonic Lodge is taking upon themselves the task that God has ordained the church to do, and yet they claim they are not a religion. Listen, my friend, a mason is going to need more than this to keep him out of the pits of hell. Adam and Eve tried to cover their sin with fig leaves and it didn't work, neither will a white leather apron. The only acceptable covering for your sins, as far as God is concerned, is the blood of Jesus Christ.

In concluding this chapter I would like to quote a Past Master, Rollin Blackmer from his book entitled The Lodge and The Craft (pp. 68-69). The following has been taken from the official monitor of the state of Alabama. It also appears in nearly the same language in the monitor published by the late General Daniel Sickels:

"It may be that in coming years upon your head will rest the laurel wreaths of victory, or from your breast hang jewels fit to grace the diadem of an Eastern potentate, nay, more than this, with Light added to coming Light your ambitious feet may tread round after round the ladder that leads to fame in our mystic circle, and even the purple of the Fraternity rest upon your honored shoulders. But never again from human hands, never again until your enfranchised spirit shall have passed upward and inward through the pearly gates shall an honor so distinguished, so emblematical of purity and all perfection be bestowed upon you as this I now confer tonight. It is yours to wear through an honorable life, and at your death, should you so will, be placed upon the coffin that contains your earthly remains and with them be laid beneath the turf and flowers. Let its fair and spotless surface be to you an ever-present reminder of a purity of life and rectitude of conduct, a never-ending argument for nobler deeds, for higher thoughts and better actions. And when at last your weary feet shall have come to the end of life's toilsome journey, and from your nerveless grasp shall drop forever the working tools of life, may the record of your actions be as pure and spotless as this fair emblem which I place in your hands tonight, and when your trembling soul shall stand before the Great White Throne, may it be your portion, my brother, to receive from the Supreme Grand Master the welcome words, "Well done, good and faithful servant, enter thou into the joy of thy Lord."

The following is attributed to Brother F. S. Elliott: "My brother, I have the pleasure of presenting to you a lambskin or white leather apron. It is the emblem of innocence and the badge of a mason, more ancient than the Golden Fleece or Roman Eagle, more honorable than the Star and Garter, when worthily worn and from a time to which the memory of man runneth not to the contrary this emblem plain and unadorned has been the peculiar clothing of all Free and Accepted Masons. The prince commanding the resources of empires and the citizen toiling in humble poverty have alike worn it with the consciousness that it has lightened the labor of the one and added dignity to the power of the other. It may be that you are, or yet will be, so firmly entrenched in the hearts of your fellowmen and so deserving of their gratitude and esteem that they will elevate you to the highest positions of trust and emolument and cause your name to be inscribed on the pillars of worldly fame, but never before have you and never again, my brother, will you have a higher mark of favor and confidence bestowed upon you than this which I, as the representative of these brethren and the craft throughout the world, am about to confer. This emblem which King Solomon wore when arrayed in all his glory, and which invested with additional dignity the immortal Washington, and which has been eagerly sought and worthily worn by the best men of your generation, I now present to you."

I have been reading and studying the Bible for nearly thirty years now, and I have never read any scripture that said or even hinted that King Solomon was ever invested with a Masonic apron, much less ever wore one.

But even if Solomon wore an apron, it sure wasn't a sign of his innocence and purity, as we can see by his later life.

He plunged into sensuality and was influenced by his many wives to introduce the worship of false gods into Jerusalem, 1 Kings 11:1-8.

His life furnishes a great warning - He is known as the wisest man, yet his wisdom did not teach him self-control. He taught well but failed to practice his own precepts. He describes the fool in the book of Proverbs and thus draws a vivid picture of his own failings.

As to the question of his repentance and of his actual end nothing positive is known. In 1 Kings 11:9-10 we read of God's anger toward Solomon - *"And the Lord was angry with Solomon, because his heart was turned from the Lord God of Israel, which had appeared unto him twice, and commanded him concerning this thing, that he should not go after other gods, but he kept not that which the Lord commanded."*

Then in verse 43 of the same chapter, we read of the death of King Solomon. Now between verse 10 and verse 43 I can find no scripture that seems to indicate to me that Solomon ever repented. Also in these verses of scripture relating to the death of Solomon, God forgot to mention that he was buried with his Masonic apron, indicating his innocence and purity of life.

Chapter 4

THE LEGEND OF HIRAM ABIFF

Edmond Ronayne in **The Master's Carpet** (pp. 339-344) says: "The following is that wonderful legend of Hiram Abiff, which is rehearsed by the Worshipful Master to every candidate at the time he is made a Master Mason, or rather after he is brought from a dead level to a living perpendicular.

Fifteen Fellow Crafts seeing the temple about to be completed and being desirous of obtaining the secrets of a Master Mason or the Master's Word whereby they might travel into foreign countries, work and receive Master's wages, entered into a horrid conspiracy to extort them from our Grand Master Hiram Abiff or take his life. But reflecting with horror upon the atrocity of the crime twelve of them recanted, the other three however, persisted in their murderous design.

Our Grand Master Hiram Abiff was slain at the hour of high twelve. It was his usual custom at that hour, while the craft were called from labor to refreshment, to enter into the unfinished "sactum sactorum" or "Holy of Holies" of King Solomon's temple, there to offer his adorations to the Deity and draw his designs upon the trestle board. The Fellow Crafts who persisted in their murderous design knowing this to be his usual custom placed themselves at the South, West and East gates of the inner court of the temple and there awaited his return.

Having finished his usual exercises he attempted to pass out by the South gate, where he was met by the first ruffian, Jubela, who thrice demanded of him the secrets of a Master Mason or Master's word and being thrice refused he struck him with the twenty-four inch gage across the throat.

He then attempted to retreat by the West gate, where he was met by the second ruffian, Jubelo, who also demanded of him the secrets of a Master Mason, or the Master's word, and being again refused he struck him with the square across the breast.

He now attempted to make his escape by the East gate, where he was met by the third ruffian, Jebelum, who in like manner thrice demanded of him the secrets of a Master Mason or the Master's word, and upon a like refusal, he struck him a violent blow with the setting maul on the forehead which felled him dead upon the spot.

They then buried him in the rubbish of the temple until low twelve or twelve at night, when they met by appointment, and conveyed him a westerly course from the temple to the brow of a hill west of Mount Moriah, where they buried him in a grave due east and west, six feet perpendicular, and planted an acacia at the head of the grave to conceal it, and that the place may be known should occasion thereafter ever require it. They then attempted to make their escape out of the country.

Our Grand Master was not known to be missing until the following day, when King Solomon arriving at the temple and finding the craft in confusion he inquired the cause, and being informed that there was not work laid out and no designs upon the trestle-board, he inquired where was our Grand Master Hiram Abiff. He was informed that he had not been seen since high twelve yesterday, and fearing that he might have been indisposed he ordered strict search and due inquiry to be made in and about the several apartments of the temple to see if he could be found. But strict search and due inquiry having already been made and our Grand Master Hiram Abiff being nowhere to be found he feared that some fatal accident had befallen him and ordered the Grand Secretary to cause the several rolls of the workmen to be called, to see if any were missing, and that return be made as speedily as possible.

Upon roll-call three Fellow Crafts were found to be missing, namely, Jubela, Jubelo, and Jubelum, who from the similarity of their names were supposed to be brethren and men of Tyre.

About that time the Fellow Crafts who had recanted presented themselves before King Solomon, clad in white gloves and aprons, tokens of innocence, freely acknowledged their premeditated guilt and most humbly implored his pardon. King Solomon ordered them to divide themselves into parties and travel three East, three West, three North and three South, (with others, whom he should appoint) in search of the ruffians and return not without tidings.

The party who pursued a westerly course from the temple, on coming down near the port of Joppa, fell in with a wayfaring man of whom they inquired if he had seen any strangers pass that way. He informed them he had, three, and described them as workmen from the temple at Jerusalem, seeking a passage to Ethiopia, but not having King Solomon's pass, were unable to obtain a passage and returned back into the country. Deeming these to be tidings of importance they returned back to communicate them.

He (King Solomon) then ordered them to disguise themselves and travel as before, with positive injunctions to find the ruffians and with as positive assurance that if they did not, the twelve Fellow Crafts would be deemed guilty of the murder and severally suffer for the crime committed.

They departed a second time and after several days of fruitless search, and when on their return one of their number, becoming more weary than the rest, sat down upon the brow of a hill west of Mount Moriah to rest and refresh himself. On attempting to arise, he accidently caught hold of an acacia, which easily giving way, excited his curiosity, whereupon he hailed his companions, and upon their return and examination found what the appearance of a new made grave. And whilst meditating upon this singular circumstance heard the following horrid exclamations from the clefts of the adjacent rock. The first was the voice of Jubela, who exclaimed, "O that my throat had been cut across, my tongue torn out by its roots and I buried in the rough sands of the sea at low water mark, where the tide ebbs and flows twice in twenty-four hours, ere I had consented to the death of so great a man as our Grand Master Hiram Abiff." The second was the voice of Jubelo, who exclaimed, "O that my left breast had been torn open, my heart plucked out and given as prey to the wild beast of the field and the fowls of the air, ere I had been accessory to the death of so good a man as our Grand Master Hiram Abiff." The third was the voice of Jubelum who exclaimed in tones of greater horror than the others, "O that my body had been severed in twain, my bowels taken from thence and burned to ashes and the ashes scattered to the four winds of heaven, so that no trace or remembrance might be had of so vile and perjured a wretch as I, ere I had caused the death of so great and so good a man as our Grand Master Hiram Abiff. Ah, Jubela and Jubelo, it is I who am more guilty than you both; it is I who struck the fatal blow, it was I who killed him." Whereupon they (the listening fellow crafts) rushed in, seized and bound them and brought them before King Solomon, who upon a due conviction and confession of their guilt ordered them to be taken without the gates of the city and be there executed according to their several imprecations whilst hidden in the clefts of the rocks.

King Solomon then ordered the Fellow Crafts to go in search of the body and when found to observe whether the Master's word or key to it or anything pertaining to the Master's degree be on or about the body. The body of our Grand Master Hiram Abiff was found in a grave dug east and west, six feet perpendicular, a westerly course from the temple, where a weary brother sat down to rest and refresh himself, but there was nothing found on or about the body, by which it could be designated, except the jewel of his office which they bore up to King Solomon.

He then ordered the Fellow Crafts to form a solemn procession to go and assist him in raising the body and as the Master's word was then lost, he proposed that the first sign made upon arriving at the grave, and the first word spoken after the body should be raised, should be adopted as the sign and word for the regulation of all Master's lodges until future generations should find out the right (word and sign)".

This, then, is the Masonic legend of Hiram Abiff, and most Blue Lodge Masons believe that it is a factual, scriptural and historical account. It is generally believed, in spite of the fact that the Masonic authorities and writers of doctrine agree that it is not only a myth, unsupported by facts, but acknowledge that it is but a retelling of the legend of Isis and Osiris. Daniel Sickels 33°, in his book **The General Ahiman Rezon** (p. 195) states: "The ceremonial of the Degree of Master Mason is unquestionably the most important, impressive, and instructive portion of the Ritual of Ancient Freemasonry.

That portion of the Rite which is connected with the legend of the Tyrian Artist, is well worthy the deep and earnest study of thoughtful men. But it should be studied as a myth, and not as a fact: and, if thus accepted, it will be found exceedingly rich in instructive lessons, and lessons, too, which admit of an immense variety of applications; whereas, if it be regarded simply as a ceremony commemorative of historical occurrences, it has no philosophical importance nor significance whatever.

Against the notion that it is the representation of a scene that actually occurred in the Temple, it may well be urged that, outside of Masonic tradition, there is no proof that an event, such as is related in connection with the Temple-Builder, ever transpired; and, besides, the ceremony is older, by more than a thousand years, than the age of Solomon. There are characters impressed upon it which cannot be mistaken it is thoroughly Egyptian."

Then, A.T.C. Pierson, Sovereign Grand Inspector General, 33°, for ten years Grand Master of the Grand Lodge of Minnesota, states in his book **Tradition of Freemasonry** (p. 240) "The Masonic legend stands by itself, unsupported by history or other than its own traditions; yet we readily recognize in Hiram Abiff, one of the Grand Masters of Freemasons, the Osiris of the Egyptians, the Mythras of the Persians, the Bacchus of the Greeks, the Dionysius of the Fraternity of the Artificers, and the Atys of the Phrygians, whose passion, death and resurrection were celebrated by these people respectively".

False religions imitate the true. Freemasonry here assures us that its model idolatries each had its murdered hero to copy and caricature the great central fact of revelation and human destiny, the death of Christ. This is the concentration of all cunning, cruelty and falsehood. Having caused, "by wicked hands," the murder of Christ, whom he could not seduce to worship himself, Satan now travesties his death for the double purpose of making the crucifixion of Christ ridiculous to those better informed by his sham counterfeits. Thus he supports his cruel throne by mischief and deceit, and drags the sons of Adam down to darkness and the pit.

L.M. McCauley in his booklet entitled **"What About Masonry"** says "The fact that The Legend Builder claims to play so important a part in sacred history, the fact that it is nowhere mentioned in any connection in Scripture, and the fact that even the central character is portrayed in a false role, all leads me to believe, that it is one of the biggest lies ever held out to a gullible world. If the outstanding character of Masonry is false and the story told and acted about him is a lie, and it is, and if Satan is the father of lies and Jesus said that he is, is not the whole fabric of the order a falsehood and Satanic? That this lie is the very foundation of the order is testified to by Albert Mackey in **Mackey's Jurisprudence** (p. 6) as follows: "The Legend of the Temple Builder constitutes the very ESSENCE and IDENTITY of Masonry."

The foundation of Masonry is the Blue Lodge with its three degrees. The highest degree in the Blue Lodge is the third, or Master's degree, and the very thing that gives this degree meaning is the legend of Hiram Abiff. It is this

Hiram, "The Widow's Son," the "Tyrian Architect", who is impersonated by every man who is initiated as a Master Mason. Because the legend of Hiram Abiff is the very foundation of all Masonry, his true identity and nature become matters of extreme importance.

The Bible informs us, that there was a person of that name employed at the building of King Solomon's temple; but neither the Bible, the writings of Josephus, nor any other writings, however ancient, of which I have any knowledge, furnish any information in respect to his last name or his death. It is very remarkable, that a man, so famous as Hiram Abiff was, an arbiter between Solomon, king of Israel, and Hiram, king of Tyre, universally acknowledged as the third most distinguished man then living, should pass off the stage of action, in the presence of King Solomon, three thousand three hundred grand overseers, and one hundred and fifty thousand workmen, with whom he had spent a number of years, and neither King Solomon, his bosom friend, nor any other among his numerous friends, even recorded his death or any thing about him.

In the lecture of the third degree, we are told, that there were "three grand masters" (Solomon, king of Israel, Hiram, king of Tyre, and Hiram Abiff") employed in building Solomon's temple. This is a fable. A grand master is master of a grand lodge. A grand lodge is composed of a number of lodges within a certain district. Where there three grand lodges in existence when the temple was built? Was there even one? The first grand lodge of which we have any record was formed in England in 1717, nearly two thousand years after the building of the temple. Anthony Sayer was the grand master of this lodge, and the first of which the history of masonry gives any account.

Sacred history gives us no information that Hiram, king of Tyre, ever left his kingdom to dwell at Jerusalem, or that he was associated with Solomon in building the temple, other than to furnish certain materials according to contract.

Hiram, the widow's son, or Masonically, "Abiff", was nothing more than a skillful workman employed by Solomon. Now by what authority do masons say that there were three grand masters associated in building the temple? These three grand masters must stand on the same list with Enoch's subterranean temple. Indeed, this degree of masonry is as great a fable as was ever invented. It is founded on the pretended death of Hiram, the widow's son. If the degree of master mason originated at the building of the temple, and was founded on the death of Hiram, then it did not exist before his death; and before this there were no master masons. But the story and the ceremony suppose that the degree did exist before, and that there was even a grand lodge at Jerusalem. If the degree did exist before his death, what was it? On what was it founded? What ceremonies did it embrace? It must have been different from what it was after. The three ruffians who are supposed to have killed Hiram, are said to have been fellow-crafts; yet the imprecation which one was heard to utter from the cave in which they were found, was the penalty attached to the oath of a master mason. What did this fellow-craft know about the oath of a master mason when he had never heard it repeated?

Hiram is said to have been killed before the temple was finished, which produced great confusion among the workmen. But the scriptures inform us that he lived to finish all the work about the temple.

1 Kings 7:40 - *"And Hiram made the lavers, and the shovels, and the basons. So Hiram made an end of doing all the work that he made king Solomon for the house of the Lord."*

The story further supposes that Hiram drew the designs and plans, and had the oversight of the building of the temple. But the scriptures inform us that the plans and designs of the temple were given Solomon by David, as he received them by the inspiration of God (I Chron. 28:11, 12 and 19); and that he had the oversight of the whole; that the business of Hiram was to prepare the vessels and furniture of the house. It is further said, that after Hiram's body had laid in the grave fourteen days, attempts were made to raise it, first by pulling the fore finger, then by pulling the second finger; last of all Solomon raised it by the master's grip. This is utterly incredible.

It is therefore certain that this degree did not originate at the building of the temple; for such things never took place as the degree supposes. It is one of the most absurd fabrications ever credited by human beings. I would like to ask professors of Christianity who feel sensitive about renouncing masonry, if they can justify themselves in giving approval to this base imposition?

Edmond Ronayne, Past Master of Keystone Lodge, No. 639 Chicago says in his book **The Master's Carpet** (pp. 148-149) "Freemasonry, casts out the name of Jesus Christ, and will not recognize him at all in any of its prayers or other acts of religious worship, while at the same time it exalts a Tyrian brass-finisher, a pagan, named Hiram Abiff, to the position of a god, magnifies his pretended virtues, extols his character, lauds his pagan piety and supposed fortitude, sings songs of praise to his name, substitutes this heathen deity for Christ, and offers freedom from sin and salvation in the "Grand Lodge above", through the mythical legend of his death and burial in the place of pardon for sin through the blood of Christ."

THE LEGEND OF ISIS AND OSIRIS

Jim Shaw in his book entitled **The Deadly Deception** (pp. 152-153) states: "It is the consensus of opinion among Masonic authorities, philosophers and writers of doctrine that the legend of Hiram Abiff is merely the Masonic version of a much older legend, that of Isis and Osiris basis of the Egyptian Mysteries. The following is a brief summary of that legend.

Osiris, sun god of the Egyptians, went on a journey to bless neighboring nations with his knowledge of arts and sciences. His jealous brother Typhon (god of winter) conspired to murder him, steal his kingdom and did so. Isis, wife of Osiris and his queen (as well as Egypt's Moon-goddess) set out on a search for the body, making inquires of all she met.

After certain adventures, she found the body with an Acacia tree at the head of the coffin. Returning home, she secretly buried the body, intending to give it a proper burial as soon as arrangements were made. Typhon, by treachery, stole the body, cut it up into fourteen pieces and hid them in as many places. Isis then made a second search and located all the pieces but one; the one missing and lost part was the phallus. She made a substitute phallus, consecrated it, and it became a sacred substitute, an object of worship. This, in extremely abbreviated form, is the Egyptian legend of Isis and Osiris. It is, without doubt, the basis for the Masonic legend of Hiram Abiff as we shall see from the following Masonic authorities themselves.

Edmond Ronayne in his book **Chapter Degrees** (pp. 125-126) wrote: "In the Master Mason's degree we are introduced to the Greater Mysteries by the alleged conflict, death, burial, and raising of Hiram Abiff, constituting, as they do, the Egyptian legend of Osiris, or Baal, without even a single change. Turning for example, to Sickel's **Freemason's Guide**, (p. 196), we are emphatically assured that Osiris and the Tyrian architect - Hiram Abiff - are one and the same, not a mortal individual, but an immortal principle."

A.T.C. Pierson in his book, **Traditions of Freemasonry** (p. 159) states: "The legend and traditions of Hiram Abiff form consummation of the connecting link between Freemasonry and the Ancient Mysteries." And in the same volume on page 34, we read: "Without doubt, Masonry originated in Pagan Sun-worship of the Oriental religions and must be traced back to Egypt, Greece, Rome and other ancient countries." Then on page 240 of the same book, Pierson states: "We readily recognize in Hiram Abiff the Osiris of the Egyptians."

The Old Testament severely condemns the worship of Baal; and Baal was a sun-god. This, therefore makes Baal and Osiris the same. And severe Judgments were sent upon the children of Israel for engaging in the rites of Baal worship. IS GOD ANY MORE PLEASED WITH BAAL WORSHIP TODAY THAN HE WAS SOME THREE THOUSAND YEARS AGO?

Albert Pike in **Morals and Dogma** (p. 476) says: "Everything good in nature comes from OSIRIS, order, harmony, and the favorable temperature of the seasons and celestial periods." Osiris was the ancient Egyptian god whose annual death and resurrection personified the self-renewing vitality and fertility of nature. "The All seeing Eye" is a Masonic representation of Osiris.

And now, in the face of all this vast accumulation of undisputed Masonic testimony, what other course is there left for us to pursue, but to believe what Freemasonry so confidently affirms concerning its own identity? When the highest Masonic authorities and leaders of the institution positively declare that its religious philosophy, its worship, and its god, are precisely the very same as existed in the "Mysteries" of Baal, in Samaria, and of Osiris, in ancient Egypt, are we going to deny it?

Edmond Ronayne in **The Master's Carpet** (pp. 239-240) says: "We must admit, whether we like it or not, that the Freemasonry of America today, both in whole and in part, is identical in every particular feature, with the secret worship of the sun-god as it was anciently practiced among pagan nations, the only difference being that the name of the hero-god is changed from Baal, or Osiris, to Hiram Abiff, and hence we must conclude whether we will, or not, that every Masonic minister is doing as much, if not more, to paganize the community and to introduce men to the idolatrous worship of Hiram, as he is to Christianize it and to bring men to the Lord Jesus Christ."

THE IMPORTANCE OF THE LEGEND

Albert Mackey 33° in his book **Symbolism of Freemasonry** (pp. 228-229) says: "The most important and significant of the legendary symbols of Freemasonry is, undoubtedly, that which relates to the fate of Hiram Abiff, commonly called," by way of excellence", the Legend of the Third Degree. The first written record that I have been able to find of this legend is contained in the second edition of Anderson's Constitutions, published in 1738, and is in these words:-"It (the temple) was finished in the short space of seven years and six months, to the amazement of all the world; when the cape-stone was celebrated by the fraternity with great joy. But their joy was soon interrupted by the sudden death of their dear master, Hiram Abiff, whom they decently interred, in the lodge near the temple, according to ancient usage."

Again Albert Mackey in **The Manual of the Lodge** (p. 99) states: "The legend of the third degree has been considered of so much importance that it has been preserved in the symbolism of every Masonic rite. No matter what modifications or alterations the general system may have undergone - no matter how much the ingenuity or the imagination of the founders of rites may have perverted or corrupted other symbols, abolishing the old, and substituting new ones - the legend of the Temple Builder has ever been left untouched, to present itself in all the integrity of its ancient mythical form.

The idea of the legend was undoubtedly borrowed from the Ancient Mysteries, where the lesson was the same as that now conveyed in the third degree of Masonry.

Viewed in this light, it is evident that it is not essential to the value of the symbolism that the legend should be proved to be historical. Whether considered as a truthful narrative of an event that actually transpired during the building of the Temple, or simply as a myth, embodying the utterance of a religious sentiment, the symbolic lesson of life and death and immortality is still contained in its teachings, and commands our earnest attention."

Carl Claudy, another well known Masonic author of at least ten books that I know of, makes the following statement in his book entitled **Introduction to Freemasonry** (p. 31) "The Legend of Hiram Abiff is at once the tragedy and the hope of man; it is virtue struck down by error, evil and sin, and raised again by truth, goodness, and mercy. It is the story of the resurrection of that which bears the nearest affinity to that supreme intelligence which pervades all nature. It is the answer to Job - "If a man dies, will he live again?"

I would like to say to Mr. Claudy as well as the other Masonic authors on this subject, that you shouldn't mix "legends and myths" with the word of God.

Jer. 23:28 - *"The prophet that hath a dream, let him tell a dream; and he that hath my word, let him speak my word faithfully."*

My friend, it isn't the Legend of Hiram Abiff that is the hope of man, but rather it is the resurrection of Jesus Christ that is the hope of man. And I might add, while I'm at it, that the resurrection of Christ isn't a "legend" either - it is one hundred percent "truth".

The belief in a resurrection to a future life as portrayed by Masonry in the third degree is not Christ-centered. In this degree the candidate is laid out "in death" and is raised from the dead by the worshipful Master of the Lodge, representing King Solomon, using the strong grip, or Lion's paw, of the Master Mason.

I would like to tell you , upon the authority of God's word, that any teaching of a resurrection outside of the power of Jesus Christ is unscriptural and a lie of the devil. Jesus says:

Matt. 28:18 - *"ALL power is given unto me in heaven and in earth,"* John 11:25 - *"Jesus said unto her, I AM the resurrection, and the life: he that believeth in me, though he were dead, yet shall he live."* 2 Cor. 4:13 - *"Knowing that he which raised up the Lord Jesus shall raise up us also BY Jesus, and shall present us with you."*

Notice here what Paul told the Corinthians, that God would raise us up, BY JESUS, not by the strong grip of the Lion's Paw.

Now on (pp.135-136) of the same book, Mr. Claudy says, speaking of the resurrection: "The lion was connected with the idea of resurrection long before the Man of Galilee walked upon the earth. In ancient Egypt as we learn from the stone carvings on the ruins of temples a lion raised Osiris from a dead level to a living perpendicular by a grip of his paw.

Judah was symbolized as a lion in his father's deathbed blessing. The lion was upon the standard of the large and powerful tribe of Judah. "Lion of the Tribe of Judah" was one of Solomon's titles.

This is another Masonic lie. Nowhere in the Bible does it say or even hint that Solomon was the "Lion of the Tribe of Judah".

Rollin Blackmer in his book **The Lodge and the Craft** (pp. 189-193) says concerning the resurrection: "Thus we close the explanation of the emblems on the solemn thought of death, which without revelation is dark and gloomy. But the good Freemason is suddenly revived by the ever-green and ever-living sprig of faith which blooms at the head of the grave. It reminds him that there is an immortal spark in man, bearing a close affinity to the Supreme Intelligence of the Universe, which shall survive beyond the grave and never, never, never die. This strengthens him to look forward with confidence and composure to a blessed immortality, and he doubts not that on the glorious morn of the Resurrection his body will rise and become as incorruptible as his soul. Then let us imitate HIRAM in his amiable and virtuous conduct, in his feigned piety to God, in his inflexible fidelity to his trust, that we may welcome the grim tyrant, Death, and receive him as a kind messenger sent by our Supreme Grand Master to translate us from this imperfect to that all perfect, glorious and Celestial Lodge above, where the Supreme Architect of the Universe presides.

Let no motive, therefore, make you swerve from your duty, violate your vows or betray your trust, but be true and faithful and imitate the example of that celebrated Artist whom you have this evening represented. Thus you will render yourself deserving of the honor which we have conferred, and worthy the confidence we have reposed in you.

Brother, you and I owe a debt of gratitude to Almighty God and thanks to the Masonic Fraternity that we stopped not, when we had taken the first or the second steps, but that being imbued with a sincere desire for more light we pressed forward and have taken the third and have at last been raised to the Sublime Degree of Master Mason; and here in our own persons enacted this symbolic resurrection".

Speaking of enacting a symbolic resurrection, the New Testament teaches that "baptism" is symbolical of the death, burial and resurrection of the Christian. Rom. 6:3 -*"Know ye not, that so many of us as were baptized into Jesus Christ were baptized into his death?"* And Col. 2:12 - *"Buried with him in baptism, wherein also ye are risen with him through the faith of the operation of God, who hath raised him from the dead."*

My friend, if the only resurrection you have ever experienced , is a Masonic resurrection, then I would like to introduce you to Jesus Christ, who is the only one that can resurrect you from the dead state of sin. Until then, you're still a ZOMBIE, a living dead person, Eph. 2:1 - *"And you hath he quickened, who were dead in trespasses and sins."* Eph. 5:14 *"Wherefore he saith, Awake thou that sleepest, and arise from the dead, and Christ shall give thee light."* Col. 2:13 - *"And you, being dead in your sins and the uncircumcision of your flesh, hath he quickened together with him, having forgiven you all trespasses."*

PERSONATING HIRAM ABIFF

Jacob O. Doesburg, Past Master of Unity Lodge, No. 191 F. and A.M. Holland, Michigan, in his book **Freemasonry Illustrated** (p. 295) tells us what the second section of the Third Degree exemplifies:

Worshipful Master - "Brother......, the second section of this degree exemplifies an instance of virtue, fortitude and integrity, seldom equaled, if ever excelled, in the history of man. You have this evening REPRESENTED one of the greatest Masons, and, perhaps, the greatest man the world ever knew, namely, our Grand Master Hiram Abiff, who was slain just before the completion of King Solomon's temple."

Daniel Sickels 33°, in his book entitled **Mystic Masonry** (p. 248) states: "Few candidates may be aware that Hiram whom they have REPRESENTED and PERSONIFIED is ideally and precisely the same as Christ. Yet such is undoubtedly the case."

Edmond Ronayne in the **Master's Carpet** (pp. 168-170) says: "In the concluding portion of the legend of the third degree, the candidate, PERSONATING Hiram Abiff, lies on the lodge floor, wound up in a canvass, shamming death. The Master and brethren surround his pretended dead body, and make two ineffectual efforts to raise it, but fail each time by reason of its supposed decomposition. The Master then, pretending to be in great distress, demands, "brethren, what shall we do?" The Senior Warden suggests, "let us pray;" the Master then adds, "brethren, let us pray;" and they all kneel on one knee, in mock solemnity around the sham dead body of the candidate - minister, Sunday School teacher, etc. - and the Master reads or repeats the following prayer:

"O God! Shield and defend us from the evil intentions of our enemies, and support us under the trials and afflictions we are destined to endure while traveling through this vale of tears. Man that is born of a woman is of few days and full of trouble. He cometh forth as a flower, and is cut down; he fleeth also as a shadow, and continueth not. O Lord have compassion on the children of thy creation, administer them comfort in time of trouble, and save them with an everlasting salvation. Amen."

Response-"So mote it be."

Now suppose that God should say to this candidate, thus enacting such a deceptive mockery, as he once said to that greedy planter, "thou fool, this moment shall thy life be required of thee," and so make him dead in reality, what would be the fearful consequence of his guilty conduct?

And if he believes at all in the teaching of God's Word, how is it possible that a minister, a Sunday School teacher or professing Christian, can retire from such a scene as this, and, kneeling in his closet, return thanks to God, through Christ, for the privilege afforded him of engaging in such a grossly, wicked abomination, and acting and personating such a lie?

ASSASSINATION OF HIRAM ABIFF

Chapter 5

UNLAWFUL AND UNCHRISTIAN NATURE OF MASONIC OATHS AND PENALTIES

It has usually been the aim of Masonic writers to present to the world the unblemished side of their institution. In this work it will be seen that a few features are presented of the dark side of the subject, which may cast a shadow over some of the "Beauties of Masonry." From what has been said in the preceding chapters, every reader must be satisfied, that the Masonic lodge is an unjustifiable association, and that its influence in some cases is harmful to the best interest of men.

The obligations or oaths which masons take upon themselves will produce the substance for discussion in this chapter. They solemnly swear to keep the secrets of masonry, and each other's secrets, and to obey the laws, rules, and regulations of the institution. Do they know the nature of these oaths before they take them? They do not; neither can they know it. They can never investigate them till after they have taken them. Is it lawful for men to take solemn oaths of which they are entirely ignorant? to swear that they will keep secrets and obey laws, yet not know what these secrets and laws may be? Herod was ignorant of the nature of his oath; it was unlawful, and he deserved to lose his life for keeping it. Masons know nothing more of the nature of their oaths before they take them than Herod did of his; and theirs is equally as unlawful. They are as ignorant of the secrets which the lodge may require them to keep, and of the laws which they may require them to obey, as Herod was of what the damsel might ask him to do. And they do not know, but it may be as unlawful for them to conceal some things which they may be ordered to, or to obey some laws which they may be required to, as it was for Herod to kill John the Baptist. They may be told by masons that the obligation is perfectly moral, and compatible with the principles of Christianity, society, and good government; but do they know this? Have they a personal knowledge of it? They have not. They only have the word of masons for it; but masons may err in judgement. After all the assurances masons can give them, and all the information they can gain from every possible source, they do not know until the oath is imposed, that it may be unlawful, or directly opposed to some other oath they may have previously taken; yet it is imposed and taken without any condition. I now present before the reader the oaths of masons, introductory to the first three degrees - known as the Blue Lodge - which I shall transcribe from Richardson's **Monitor of Free-Masonry**.

As soon as the candidate is placed in position, the Worshipful Master approaches him, and says - Mr. Smith, you are now placed in a proper position to take upon you the solemn oath or obligation of an **Entered Apprentice Mason**, which I assure you is neither to affect your religion or your politics. If you are willing to take it, repeat your name and say after me.

FIRST OATH -"I, John Smith, of my own free will and accord, in presence of Almighty God, and this worshipful Lodge of Free and Accepted Masons, dedicated to God and held forth to the holy order of St. Johns, do hereby and hereon most solemnly and sincerely promise and swear, that I will always hail, ever conceal, and never reveal any part or parts, art or arts, point or points of the secrets, arts and mysteries of ancient Free Masonry, which I have received, am about to receive, or may hereafter be instructed in, to any person or persons in the known world, except it be a true and lawful brother Mason, or within the body of a just and lawfully constituted lodge of such, and not unto him, nor unto them whom I shall hear so to be, but unto him and them only whom I shall find so to be, after strict trial and due examination or lawful information. Furthermore do I promise and swear, that I will not write, print, stamp, stain, hew, cut, carve, indent, paint, or engrave it on anything moveable or immovable, under the whole canopy of heaven, whereby, or whereon the least letter, figure, character, mark, stain, shadow, or resemblance of the same may become legible or intelligible to myself or any other person in the known world, whereby the secrets of Masonry may be unlawfully obtained through my unworthiness. To all which I do most solemnly and sincerely promise and swear, without the least equivocation, mental reservation, or self evasion of mind in me whatever; binding myself under no less penalty than to have my throat cut across, my tongue torn out by the roots, and my body buried in the rough sands of the sea at low water mark, where the tide ebbs and flows twice in twenty-four hours; so help me God, and keep me steadfast in the due performance of the same."

SECOND OATH - "I, John Smith, of my own free will and accord, in the presence of Almighty God and this worshipful Lodge of Fellow Craft Masons, erected to God, and dedicated to the holy order of St. Johns, do hereby and hereon most solemnly and sincerely promise and swear, in addition to my former obligation, that I will not give the secrets of the degree of a Fellow Craft Mason to any one of an inferior degree, nor to any other being in the known world, except it be to a true and lawful brother, or brethren Fellow Craft Mason, or within the body of a just and lawfully constituted Lodge of such; and not unto him nor unto them whom I shall hear so to be, but unto him and unto them only whom I shall find so to be, after strict trial and due examination, or lawful information. Furthermore, do I promise and swear, that I will not knowingly wrong this lodge, nor a brother of this degree, to the value of two cents, myself, nor suffer it to be done by others, if in my power to prevent it. Furthermore, do I promise and swear, that I will support the constitution of the Grand Lodge of the United States, and of the Grand lodge of this State, under which this Lodge is held, and conform to all the by-laws, rules, and regulations of this or any other Lodge, of which I may, at any time hereafter, become a member. Furthermore, do I promise and swear, that I will obey all regular signs and summonses given, handed, sent, or thrown to me by the hand of a brother Fellow Craft Mason, or from the body of a just and lawfully constituted Lodge of such; provided it be within the length of my cable-tow, or a square and angle of my work. Furthermore, do I promise and swear, that I will be aiding and assisting all poor and indigent brethren Fellow Crafts, their widows and orphans, wheresoever dispersed round the globe, they applying to me as such, and I finding them worthy, as far as in my power, without injuring myself or family. To all of which, I do most solemnly and sincerely promise and swear, without any hesitation, mental reservation, or self-evasion of mind in me whatever, binding myself under no less penalty than to have my left breast torn open, my heart and vitals taken from thence, thrown over my left shoulder, and carried to the valley of Jehosaphat, there to become a prey to the wild beasts of the field, and vultures of the air, should I willfully violate, or transgress any part of this, my solemn oath or obligation, of a Fellow Craft Mason. So help me God, and keep me steadfast in the due performance of the same."

THIRD OATH - "I, John Smith, of my own free will and accord, in the presence of Almighty God, and this worshipful lodge of Master Masons, erected to God and dedicated to the holy St. Johns, do hereby and hereon, most solemnly and sincerely promise and swear, in addition to my former obligations, that I will not give the secrets of a Master Mason to any one of an inferior degree, nor to any being in the known world, except it be to a true and lawful brother Master Mason, or within the body of a just and lawfully constituted Lodge of such; and not unto him or them whom I shall hear so to be, but unto him and them only whom I shall find so to be, after strict trial, due examination, or lawful information received. Furthermore, do I promise and swear, that I will not speak the Master Mason's word, which I shall hereafter receive, in any other manner except in that in which I shall receive it, which will be on the five points of fellowship, and at low breath. Furthermore do I promise and swear, that I will not give the grand hailing sign of distress of this degree, except I am in real distress, or for the benefit of the craft, when at work; and should I see that sign given, or hear the words accompanying it, I will fly to the relief of the person so giving it, should there be a greater probability of saving his life than losing my own. Furthermore do I promise and swear, that I will not wrong this Lodge, nor a brother of this degree, to the value of one cent knowingly, myself, nor suffer it to be done by others, if in my power to prevent it. Furthermore do I promise and swear, that I will not be at the initiating, passing, or raising a candidate at one communication without a dispensation from the Grand Lodge, for that purpose. Furthermore do I promise and swear, that I will not be at the initiating, passing, or raising a candidate in a clandestine Lodge, nor converse upon the secrets of Free Masonry with a clandestine made Mason, or one that has been expelled or suspended, while he is under that sentence. Furthermore do I promise and swear, that I will not be at the initiating, passing, or raising of an old man in dotage, a young man in non-age, an atheist, irreligious libertine, madman, hermaphrodite, woman, or a fool. Furthermore do I promise and swear, that I will not speak evil of a brother Master Mason, neither behind his back nor before his face, but will apprise him of all approaching danger. Furthermore do I promise and swear, that I will not violate the chastity of a Master Mason's wife, mother, sister, or daughter, nor suffer it to be done by others, if in my power to prevent it, I knowing them to be such. Furthermore do I promise and swear, that I will support the constitution of the Grand Lodge of this State, under which this Lodge is held, and conform to all the by-laws, rules and regulations of this, or any other Lodge of which I may hereafter become a member. Furthermore do I promise and swear, that I will obey all due signs and summonses handed, sent, or thrown to me from a brother Master Mason, or from the body of a just and lawfully constituted Lodge of Master Masons, if within the length of my cable-tow. Furthermore do I promise and swear, that a Master Mason's secrets, given to me in charge as such, shall remain as secure and inviolable in my breast, as in his, before communicated, murder and treason only excepted; and they left to my only election. Furthermore do I promise and swear, that I will go on a Master Mason's errand, even barefoot, and bareheaded, to save his life, or relieve his necessities. Furthermore do I promise and swear, that I will remember a brother Master Mason, when on my knees at my devotions. Furthermore do I promise and swear, that I will be aiding and assisting all poor and indigent Master Masons, their widows and orphans, wheresoever dispersed round the globe, (they making application to me as such, and I finding them worthy), as far as in my power, without injury to myself or family. Furthermore do I promise and swear, that if any part of this my solemn oath or obligation be omitted at this time, that I will hold myself amenable thereto, whenever informed. To all which I do most solemnly and sincerely promise and swear, with a fixed and steady purpose of mind in me to keep and perform the same, binding myself under no less penalty than to have my body severed in two in the midst, and divided to the North and South, my bowels burnt to ashes in the center, and the ashes scattered before the four winds of heaven, that there might not the least tract or trace of remembrance remain among men or Masons of so vile and perjured a wretch as I should be, were I ever to prove willfully guilty of violating any part of this my solemn oath or obligation of a Master Mason; so help me God, and keep me steadfast in the due performance of the same."

Doesn't it surprise you that men of sense and of professed piety, should bow down in the presence of God, and take upon them such obligations, and then jealously defend the corrupt system which they support? These oaths are unlawful and unchristian.

What authority do masons have to administer them? To administer oaths is office work, and belongs to none but to those who are duly authorized by the constituted authorities of the land. Oaths administered by masons are as illegal as if administered by any private citizen. The administration of extrajudicial oaths, is what our free government does not authorize. The first step is therefore illegal.

They have no authority to administer oaths, much more to administer them under the penalty of death. For, should they be violated, from what source will they receive a commission to execute their penalties? Must a man, for a mere breach of confidence, or for the violation of an oath which has never been sanctioned by the laws of his country, die the most infamous death? If the violation of these oaths were perjury, (which they are not) must a man die for perjury? What law of any civilized nation, ever said, that a man, should have his throat cut, his tongue torn out by the roots, and his body buried in the rough sands of the sea, for such an offense? The penalties connected to these oaths are inhuman and would make a cannibal blush. No human butcher would mutilate a hog, the way these masons consent to have their bodies mutilated. No Christian has a right to put up his life as a pledge. We read in the bible - "Ye are not your own." I might just as well rob a bank, and put that up as a pledge, as to pledge my life, which does not belong to me. 1 Cor. 6:19-20 - *"What? Know ye not that your body is the temple of the Holy Ghost which is in you, which ye have of God, and ye are not your own? For ye are bought with a price: therefore glorify God in your body, and in your spirit, which are God's."*

Certainly Masonic oaths, if taken at face value, mean that masonry assumes the right to have assassinated those whom they may count as traitors. It is foolishness, in the extreme, to suppose that an organized body of men, should, in the presence of Almighty God, administer laws which they do not intend to execute. These oaths are fundamental laws, which are administered by the Masonic society; all that is dear to its own existence supposes that they are pledged to execute them when violated. Death is the penalty; and if it is not their intention to execute it, the institution is the greatest piece of mockery that ever existed.

Masonry is a murderous institution, because it is based on laws which require murder. Those laws which support the system, demand the life of a fellow creature, without any reference to the laws of God or country; but contrary to both. Put an end to these laws, and the whole framework of the organization would collapse. Who then does not see, that the very principles, spirit, and essence, of this ancient fraternity, are murderous!

Those who join the lodge, solemnly swear that, if they violate "any part" of their oaths, they will submit to be executed in the manner the oaths prescribe. Should a Christian, calling on Almighty God to bear him witness, offer himself and bind himself for any such penalties on the body, which is purchased by the blood of Christ on the cross, and which is indwelt by the Holy spirit, and do all that lest he should reveal some of the silly so-called secrets of masonry which are widely published and available for anyone who has the money to purchase them? But if it is wicked and unchristian for a man to bind himself and offer his body for this murderous mutilation, then is it right for the lodge to administer the oath and assess the penalty, calling upon God to see it fulfilled? What group of men has the right to murder for the protection of their secret rituals? And every oath with such a penalty assumes that the lodge has a right to execute the penalty and the duty to do it. Oaths vary in the different degrees of the Masonic order. In one degree, the drama is enacted of a man seen peeping who is discovered and seized and sentenced to death as an example of what is to happen to one so indiscreet as to divulge his obligations. The explanation says, "we are bound to cause their DEATH, and take vengeance on the treason by the destruction of the traitors."

What a disgrace to the dignity of man; that in this land of bibles, and blood bought independence, a society should exist which claims the prerogative of sacrificing human beings, without any reference to the God of the bible, or to the laws of our boasted freedom! Such, I am not hesitant to say, is the Masonic society. Yet, many, who name the name of Christ, are Sunday school teachers, and ministers of the gospel, are enrolled on its list, and are lending their influence to support it.

What must be the feelings of a Christian, to administer such oaths? In what light would he appear to execute any of the penalties? Could he do this in the fear of God? Could he in cold blood, lay hands on a brother, and cut his throat, and tear out his tongue, or tear open his breast and take out his heart and vitals; or cut his body in two and burn his bowels to ashes; and then say, "I have done the duty of a Christian?" Even if he does not do this himself, in case of a violation, he is bound to give his approval to it, when done by others, or renounce the institution.

In view of the nature of these oaths, we may easily account for the outrageous disposition which some masons often manifest. It is produced and nourished, by the uncivilized doctrines which lie at the foundation of their system. This disposition is necessary to qualify them to defend the institution. Could they call in the aid of the "powers that be," those who dare to oppose them, and to investigate their system, would be compelled to flee before the storm of Masonic wrath. In a society, which prohibits, on pain of death, a full and fair investigation of all its principles, may we not take it for granted, that these principles are corrupt, and their influence dangerous? Such a society, was never originated by men who professed the religion of the bible, and the politics of a free government.

MASONIC OATHS OPPOSED TO GOOD GOVERNMENT AND LAW

I wish to say that the Masonic oaths are at variance with good government and opposed to law and order. And since the bible teaches, in Rom.13:1-4, that civil government is ordained of God, this once again brings them into conflict with the bible. The oaths of lodge members which bind them to help other lodge members in almost any circumstances, and in some cases without exception, present a great political danger to the nation. As an example, I would like to quote a part of the oath or obligation, taken by a Royal Arch Mason, from a "Ritual of Freemasonry" (p. 115) published by Wm. Reeves - "I further promise and swear, that I will assist a companion Royal Arch Mason, when I see him engaged in any difficulty, and will espouse his cause so far as to extricate him from the same, whether he be RIGHT or WRONG."

It should further be noted that in the Royal Arch Degree, the candidate swears to protect the "brethren", **murder and treason not excepted**. This places the Masonic oath above that of our courts and our country. What chance would you have against a mason in a criminal or civil court with a Judge who is a 32nd or 33rd degree mason? None, by the nature of their oaths. The obligation to assist another so far as to extricate him from difficulty, whether he be right or wrong, and to conceal another's secrets, even though those secrets should involve the highest and most enormous crimes, is most assuredly opposed to the spirit of the gospel, and to the pure system of morality spoken of therein. And to call upon Almighty God to give sanction to such obligations is, in my opinion, the height of blasphemy. Now, is this right? Is this consistent with duty, either to God or man? Must not this often prove a fatal bar to the detection of crime, and the administration of justice? What is the moral character of a man who does all he can to rescue a criminal from the hands of justice? Lodge oaths tend to protect criminals, defeat justice and make lodge members into liars and deceivers. Is there nothing unchristian in this oath? May the children of God solemnly swear, that they will keep the secrets of drunkards, profane swearers, thieves, robbers, adulterers, kidnapers, rapist, or any others? This oath requires masons to conceal everything - crimes of every description when given to each other as secrets, including murder and treason.

Suppose two men are masons; one is guilty of some crime, which he tells to the other as a secret; no matter what, if it includes murder; he is under oath never to reveal it. The criminal is caught, his friend is called upon as a witness against him, and solemnly swears in the presence of Almighty God to tell the whole truth. He is guilty of false swearing. If he tells the whole truth, he has violated his Masonic oath; if he doesn't tell the truth, he has violated his civil oath. No matter which direction he chooses to take, he has sworn falsely. What confidence can we have in such men, though they may make high professions? This oath destroys the foundation of confidence; which in any person, is that truthfulness which affords a pledge, that on every lawful occasion, he will invariably tell "the truth, the whole truth, and nothing but the truth." But the above oath solemnly forbids this; and if it were taken by all men, would sweep from the world the foundation of justice and of social order.

As this oath does not on all occasions, allow masons to give the truth in evidence against a brother, how can those who are not masons obtain compensation for injuries which they may receive? Let a mason commit the most harmful aggression upon the property or character of his neighbor, let this cause be brought before a court of justice, let another mason, to whom the criminal has committed the whole affair as a secret, be called as a witness against him, and the oath which he has taken, decidedly forbids that he should offer his testimony. Should he be the only witness in the case, the innocent might suffer, and the guilty escape. Such a society, embracing so many men who are inclined to act wickedly, endangers the dearest rights of peaceable and honest citizens. There may be many circumstances in which it would be impossible for them to obtain the justice of their cause. A shelter is afforded to the worst of men, behind which they may withdraw, and invent and execute their dark and secret plots of destruction and deceit, perfectly unknown to others; and the oaths and obligations into which they have entered, puts them beyond the reach of the law, where no civil process can detect them. The fundamental truths of the institution have been kept so much behind the curtain, that few have ventured to investigate them and to expose them to the public, so that most men are not aware of the danger to which their civil and religious rights are exposed.

How must this oath clash with the obligations of a Christian? Suppose two masons are church members, one is guilty of a crime which he relates to the other as a secret; the church calls him to an account, and the other is called as a witness against him; all that is solemn in his covenant with God and his brethren, demands of him to tell the whole truth; but he has sworn not to do it. The Masonic oath and his Christian obligations are at war, one or the other has to be violated.

If there is trouble between these two masons; their obligations as masons require them to settle it in the lodge, but their obligations as Christians require them to settle it in the church. Now if one brother has a complaint against the other, to whom does the bible direct him to tell it - to the lodge? No, to the church. If he goes to any other tribunal, he violates the law of Christ. But his obligations as a mason, require him to go to the lodge, and if he does not, he violates the discipline of the lodge. For this reason, it appears as clear as day, that no man can perform the duties of a mason and of a Christian, at the same time.

A mason's obligations, so far as they clash with other obligations are unlawful, and are not binding; for no obligation can bind a man to practice what is unlawful. For this reason, so far as his duty to God and his fellowmen requires him to break his obligations as a mason, so far is he bound to do it. No man can serve two masters; and it is better to obey God than the lodge.

It is the duty of every person who has taken these oaths, to renounce them, and to confess his wrong in taking them. It is wrong to take them; it is a greater wrong to keep them. They are binding on no human being. Was the oath of Herod binding? If it were there was no crime in his beheading of John the Baptist. He did his duty. If Masonic oaths are binding, then it is the duty of all who have taken them to reduce them to practice. Therefore, should one mason conceal the crimes of another before the courts of justice, because of his oath, he will do right. Should the members of a court, who are masons, use their influence to free the criminal before them, because he is a mason, and gives the sign of distress, they will do right. Should any mason violate these oaths, and should his brethren execute him in the manner the oaths prescribe, they will do right. If Masonic oaths are binding, this course of reasoning is unavoidable.

These oaths are at no time taken understandingly. The candidate never reads them, nor hears them repeated before he takes them, consequently has never investigated them. As to their nature and tendency, he is entirely in the dark, until he is solemnly bound. The candidate repeats them after the Worshipful Master, sentence by sentence, and this is the first time he ever hears them, or has any correct information about them. Every one should be able to see, that they are taken in a careless manner. Had they been presented to the public for a full and fair investigation, very few would ever had taken them.

In taking these oaths, two wrongs may be observed. First - in the candidate; who, in an inconsiderate manner, rushes into the presence of God, and swears about something of which he is entirely ignorant of. This is highly criminal. No man can be justified in taking a solemn oath, without having first examined its nature. If he is not permitted to do this, then he may well suspicion that there is danger ahead. But to venture forward and make a solemn promise before God, of the nature of which he knows nothing, is presumption in the extreme. Secondly - there is a wrong in those who administer the oaths; they know that the candidate is ignorant of the solemn vows which he is about to make; and they have good reason to believe, that if he were not, he would never consent to make them. It is their policy to keep him ignorant until he is placed where it will be difficult, if not dangerous, to retract. They practice the most glaring deception - they tell the candidate that the obligations are perfectly "moral and compatible with the principles of Christianity, civil society, and good government." When he is about to take any of the oaths, the Worshipful Master says to him, "I assure you it is neither to affect your religion nor your politics." These assurances, though often given by men of high professions, are false and deceptive. Every person professing the salvation of the bible and the politics of a free government, must know that the oaths which masons take, seriously affect both. These oaths which the candidate consents to take, and which masons profess to administer to him, are not to affect either. If they do, they are not binding, because they are of a different nature from what he anticipated. He has been deceived. He is not only justifiable in renouncing them, but criminal if he does not. His ignorance, the inconsiderate manner in which he takes them, the deception and falsehood practiced by the institution, together with their unlawful, unchristian, and even savage nature, require him to renounce them immediately. They are as much in contrast with the holy precepts of the gospel of Jesus, as light is with darkness. When a candidate puts confidence in those who instruct him, and takes upon him obligations, or makes promises, which, when he is permitted to examine for himself he finds are of a different nature from what he was told by the other party they would be - right there and then, they become null and void. No judicial or ecclesiastical investigation can incriminate him for renouncing them. After all, it would be far better to obey the solemn injunction of the Saviour, "But I say unto you, swear not at all."

Chapter 6

OBLIGATIONS IN SOME OF THE HIGHER DEGREES

We will now examine the nature of the obligations which are administered in some of the higher degrees of masonry, as taken from **Freemasonry Illustrated**, by Jacob 0. Doesburg, Past Master of Unity Lodge No. 191, F. & A .M., Holland, Michigan. **Royal Arch Degree** - "Furthermore do I promise and swear, that I will aid and assist a companion royal arch mason wherever I shall see him engaged in any difficulty, so far as to extricate him from the same, **whether he be right or wrong**." If a royal arch mason is guilty of theft, arson, treason, murder, or any other crime, is apprehended and faces a due reward according to the laws of his state, his royal arch brethren who see him engaged in this difficulty, are bound by their oath to "aid and assist," so far as to extricate him from it - to free him from the grasp of justice and turn him loose again upon the world. If a member of the church, who is a royal arch mason, gets in difficulty in the church, his royal arch brethren of the church are bound to assist him, **"right or wrong;"** and if they cannot extricate him otherwise, to oppose, and if possible to defeat every righteous effort made by the church to discipline him.

"Furthermore do I promise and swear, that a companion royal arch mason's secrets, given to me in charge as such, and I knowing him to be such, shall remain as secure and inviable in my breast as in his own, when communicated to me, **murder** and **treason** NOT excepted." How many professed ministers of Christ have taken this oath? These men preach, that "without holiness no man shall see the Lord," nevertheless have solemnly sworn that they will conceal the crimes of a traitor or murderer, and even aid and assist him to escape detection and the justice of the law to extricate him from his difficulty "whether he be right or wrong." Should they be called to testify against this royal arch traitor or murderer, whose crimes they have been charged to conceal, the oath, if they consider it binding, must close their lips; or if they swear, they must swear falsely - that they have no knowledge of his crimes. They must swear thus, not only to keep his secrets, but to extricate him from his difficulty. It is nonsense to swear that they will conceal such crimes among themselves, if it is not expected that they will ever be guilty of them. And if they do commit them - if they stain their hands with the blood of their fellow men - if they conspire to overthrow the liberties of their country - if they do these things repeatedly, they are not to be exposed, but held and treated as members in good standing. Men, (no matter what title they wear), who will conceal murder and treason, and assist criminals to escape punishment, cannot safely be intrusted with any office connected with the administration of the law. Suppose he is a police officer, a sheriff, or a state patrolman. Will he not be able to prevent the execution of justice, if he does all within his power, to extricate his brethren, as he has solemnly sworn to do?

The penalties attached to the laws of God and the state, are designed to discourage, and in many cases do discourage men from crime; but this oath is directly calculated to do away with these barriers - to defeat the government of God and our country - to turn man loose upon his fellow men without any restraint. While this oath is taken and adhered to by a powerful society existing in the midst of us, members of which are often intrusted with high and responsible offices, it will be utterly impossible to maintain righteous government. If a royal arch mason commits a crime, there is little fear of his being detected; and even if he should be, his brethren, who perhaps are the judge and members of the jury, to whose hands he will be committed as a criminal, are solemnly bound, under no less penalty than "to have their skulls struck off and their brains exposed to the scorching rays of the sun," not only to conceal his crimes, but to assist him so far as to put him beyond the reach of punishment - to extricate him from his difficulty, "whether he is right or wrong." Where is the safety of our property, our liberties, our lives, and of our boasted free constitution!

A royal arch mason "swears to vote for a companion royal arch mason, before any other person of equal qualifications". It has often been said, that most of the important offices are held by masons. This is undoubtedly true, and the reason why is because of their oaths. It can no longer be said with any propriety, that masonry has no influence in politics; for we have the clearest proof (from their own publishing house) that it is a powerful engine in the political world, and has long been a stepping stone to places of honor, profit, and power. I have a book in my library published by Macoy Publishing & Masonic Supply Co., entitled "**10,000 Famous Freemasons**," by William R. Denslow. This book is volume one, contains 339 pages, and list alphabetically the last names of individuals starting with the letter A thru D, and list their titles or political office, etc. In volume one alone I counted no less than 219 Governors, 135 Senators, 150 Congressmen, 26 Admirals and Rear Admirals, 158 Generals of the Army, Air Force, and Marines, 51 Chief Justices of the Supreme Court, and 83 Justices of the Supreme Court. Also it listed a certain number of Surgeon Generals, Postmaster Generals, U.S. District Judges, Ambassadors, and Secretaries of State, etc., etc.

By the influence of these Masonic oaths the worst of men may be thrust into office - men who will not hesitate a moment to violate their civil oaths of office to preserve the "ancient landmarks of the order," or to "extricate a brother from his difficulty, whether he is right or wrong."

The penalties annexed to the oath of knights of the red cross - "Binding myself under no less penalty than that of having my house torn down, the timber thereof set up and I hanged thereon, and when the last trump shall blow, that I be forever excluded from the society of all true and courteous knights, should I ever willfully and knowingly violate any part of this solemn obligation." The oath supposes that all true and courteous knights are saved; for the candidate swears afterwards, "to put confidence in every illustrious brother of the cross as a true and worthy follower of the blessed Jesus." Now to swear that he will be forever excluded from the society of the "true and worthy followers of the blessed Jesus," is to swear that he will be forever excluded from heaven - will forever suffer the pains of hell, as the penalty of the oath.

Similar to this is what is called the "sealed obligation," (See Foldout), in which, when the candidate drinks wine from a human skull, he swears - "As the sins of the whole world were laid upon the head of the Saviour, so may all the sins committed by the person whose skull this was, be heaped upon my head in addition to my own, should I ever knowingly or willfully violate or transgress any obligation that I have heretofore taken, take at this time, or shall at any future period take, in relation to any degree of masonry or order of knighthood. So help me God". Here the candidate swears, that should he violate any oath which he may take in masonry, or knighthood, from first to last, he will suffer the punishment due for his own sins and for the sins of another. How many members of churches and professed ministers of Christ, have taken this horrible oath; bound themselves under no less penalty than the eternal, and even double torments of the damned, that they will keep the secrets of the order! What an appalling evidence of human depravity! What can be more awful! The salvation of the candidate is wholly dependent on the keeping of these Masonic oaths. The whole mediation of the Son of God is sworn away! One would think that the heart of a good man on this occasion, drinking wine from a human skull, swearing away his blessed Lord - binding himself under endless sufferings to keep the secrets of a corrupt and wicked institution, would die within him! Man sinks low indeed when he is so wicked as to call upon God to help him and to keep him steadfast in breaking his commandments and keeping these ungodly oaths. Don't tell me masonry does not profess to be a religion; when according to some of the oaths administered, the salvation of those who take them, depend wholly on masonry - is wholly dependent on keeping every part of every oath taken from first to last.

A knight Templar swears - "Furthermore do I promise, that I will wield my sword in defence of innocent virgins, destitute widows, helpless orphans, and the Christian religion." Is this the way Christians are to promote the good of their fellow men - of those who are in affliction? The bible directs us to "visit the fatherless and widows in their affliction and keep himself unspotted from the world." Is this the way they are to promote their religion? Are ministers of the meek and lowly Jesus, to carry the bible in one hand and the sword in the other? This is the doctrine on which is based the profane system and bloody conquests of Mahomet. Who would have thought, that there were men in this enlightened country of ours, and even ministers of the gospel, who have bound themselves under tremendous curses, to fight with carnal weapons in defence of their religion? "Our weapons", says the apostle, "are not carnal, but mighty through God to the pulling down of strong holds".

An illustrious knight - "You further swear that should you ever know a companion to violate any essential part of this obligation, you will use your most decided endeavors, by the blessing of God, to bring such a person to the strictest and most condign punishment, agreeable to the rules and usages of our ancient fraternity; and this by pointing him out to the world as an unworthy and vicious vagabond, by opposing his interest, by deranging his business, by transferring his character after him wherever he may go, by exposing him to the contempt of the whole fraternity and the world, but more especially to our illustrious order, during his whole natural life." Now according to the rules and usages of the ancient fraternity, traitors were put to death as I have shown before. Professors of Christianity who take this oath, swear, that if any one of the order, though a brother in the church, should, from a sense of duty, expose their profane mysteries to the world, I say, they solemnly swear, "in the dread presence of the most holy and Almighty God," that they will use their most decided endeavors to put him to death - to bring him to condign punishment according to the rules of the ancient fraternity, when those who violated their oaths were, by order of the grand master, executed according to the imprecations of their own mouths - received a punishment adequate to their crimes. Should they not think it prudent to put him to death, they swear to **"point him out to the world as an unworthy and vicious vagabond"**. "Though his character as a neighbor, a citizen, a Christian and a minister, stands unblemished and high, and his praise is in all the churches; yet they solemnly swear, that by the tongue of slander and deceit, they will destroy his character, sink his reputation and hold him up to the world as an outcast - as unfit for human society. To do this, they must invent and circulate falsehoods. They therefore swear, in substance, that they will spread slanderous reports concerning a professed brother in Christ, for the avowed purpose of ruining his character and of pointing him out to the world as a "vicious vagabond." Compare this with the bible - "Speak not evil, one of another brethren." - "Speak evil of no man." - "What shall be given unto thee, or what shall be done unto thee thou false tongue?"

The worthy minister of Christ, or any other person, having incurred the displeasure of that illustrious order, by exposing their wickedness, is not permitted to sustain an honest character if their slanderous tongues can destroy it; nor to possess a lawful interest if their wicked hand can overthrow it. What civilized men, and even professors of Christianity, would join together by solemn oaths to oppose a brother's lawful interest? Is this the spirit of Christianity? Is it not that of the infernal regions? "Let no man seek his own but every man another's wealth," is a divine requirement.

What laws has he broken? Has he violated the laws of God? They say - "Let him enjoy no happiness while he is within reach of Masonic VENGEANCE. What a contrast between this oath and the precepts of the gospel! "Thou shalt love thy neighbor as thyself." "Love worketh no ill to his neighbor." "Do good to all men." "Love your enemies, bless them that curse you, do good to them that hate you,"

A church member who takes the following oath, cast away the solemn covenant which he has entered into with God and his people - "In dread presence of the most holy and Almighty God, I solemnly swear and declare, that I will give myself forever to this holy and illustrious order." The man who takes this obligation and holds himself bound by it, cannot with any propriety be acknowledged as a member of the church of God.

Once more hear these illustrious knights swear -"I swear to look on his enemies as my enemies, and his friends as my friends, and stand forth to mete out tender kindness or vengeance accordingly." No matter whether "he is right or wrong;" his enemies shall be my enemies and his friends my friends. If the best of men are his enemies, they shall be my enemies: if the worst of men are his friends they shall be my friends. "And will stand forth to mete out **vengeance** accordingly." Have these illustrious beings - these dealers in VENGEANCE, never read the following scripture - "VENGEANCE IS MINE, and I will repay, saith the Lord." If a man in the defence of a righteous cause - for the promotion of truth and the advancement of the kingdom of God, provokes the ill will of an individual sir knight, he is exposed to the wrath of ALL sir knights. They will unitedly "stand forth and mete out **vengeance**" to him. He may expect to be pointed out to the world as an "**unworthy and vicious vagabond**". Here in these United States where we have enjoyed freedom and liberty, are planted the poisonous seeds of sedition and anarchy. Where is the man who is so in love with wickedness and suffering, so lost to the safety of his own character, liberty and country - where is the Christian, the minister of God, so indifferent to the purity of the church and the honor of his divine Master, as not to use his greatest efforts by the blessing of God, to bring this illustrious order, (not to "**condign punishment**") but into oblivion? Men, who are acquainted with the nature of masonry, and still maintain a connection with it, must in the future stand no higher in the esteem of a judicious public, than conspirators against all law, human and divine.

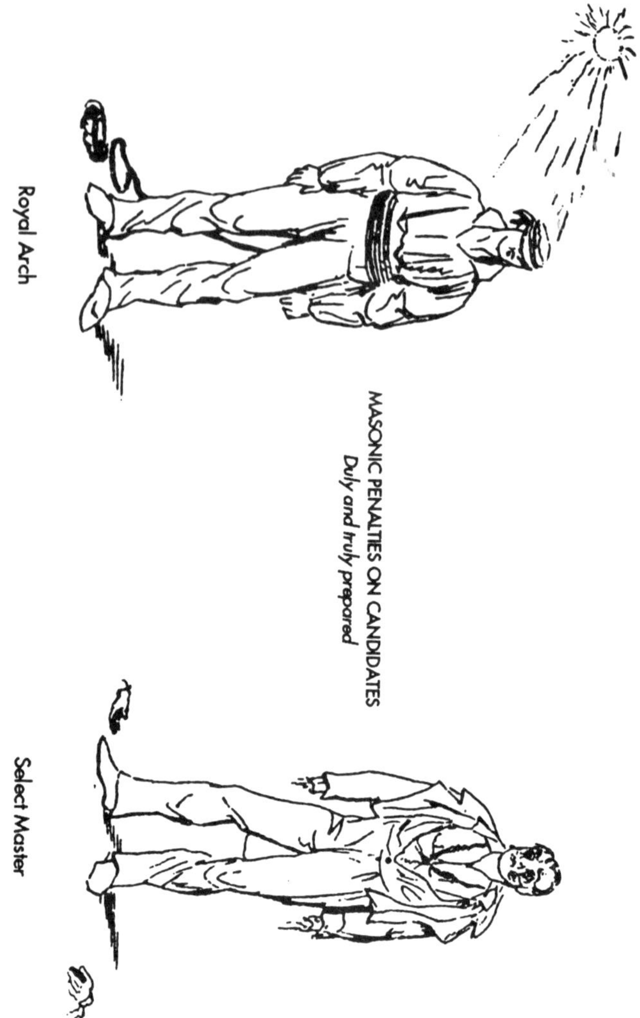
MASONIC PENALTIES ON CANDIDATES
Duly and truly prepared
Royal Arch
Select Master

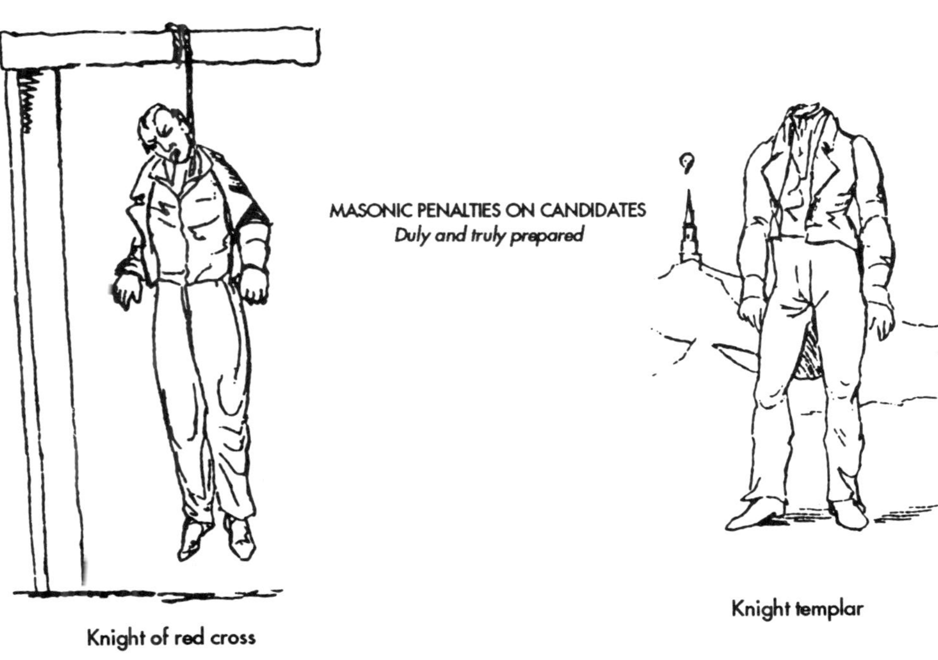

MASONIC PENALTIES ON CANDIDATES

Duly and truly prepared

Knight of red cross

Knight templar

MASONIC PENALTIES ON CANDIDATES

Duly and truly prepared

Heroine of Jericho

Secret monitor

Chapter 7

MASONIC LAW REQUIRES THE TAKING OF HUMAN LIFE

In the ritualistic ceremonies, the question is asked, "What makes you a mason? The answer is, "My oath." The oath then is the most important part of masonry. If it doesn't mean anything, and is just idle words, then men are taking seriously what they will be brought into judgment for-idle words. (Matt. 12:36-37). If the oath means anything, then every mason is a potential murderer. In this work, I have attempted to show from the nature of Masonic oaths, that the institution is based on laws which require the taking of human life, contrary to the laws of God and country. Members of the lodge frequently deny this, and say that the oaths and penalties are just symbolical and not real. If that is true, then may I ask - what are they symbolical of? In the 30th degree, the candidate himself inflicts the penalty of the oath by stabbing in effigy the King and the Pope. Why does the candidate actually act this out if it is only symbolical? Furthermore, the oath is supposed to be taken before God. Is God a part to such things? Does God require a man to bind himself under a death penalty to keep certain unimportant things secret? Admitting, say they, that the candidate binds himself under those horrible penalties, no one is bound to execute them in case of an offense. As this is an important point, and as much depends on its being put beyond the reach of controversy, it may be well to offer further remarks upon it at this time.

If no one is bound to execute the penalties, then the candidate is at liberty to reveal masonry, without exposing himself any more than he would if the solemn mockery of administering the oaths had never taken place. If he is not bound by the penalties to keep the oaths, then the oaths are nothing. If the penalties are a sham, the oaths are a sham, and no part of them is binding. If masons in administering them do not intend to place the candidate fully under their penalties, then they do not intend to place him under the promissory part of them. Will they abide by this? Has the subject generally been understood in this light either by themselves or by others?

But let us appeal to the conduct of the institution, as it is said to be handed down from ancient time by traditions and ceremonies. By these traditions and ceremonies, on which some of the degrees are founded, they teach the candidate that it was their ancient custom to execute those who violated their obligations and became traitors.

The three ruffians who are said to have killed Hiram Abiff, were apprehended and executed in strict accordance with the penalties of the oaths, "according to the several imprecations of their own mouths." This was done by the institution - by order of the grand master. Will it be said that they were murderers, and according to the law of God deserved to die? But what authority had Solomon, as grand master of masons, to execute murders? They were not executed according to the law of God as murderers, but according to Masonic law and Masonic authority. These bloody scenes are the foundation of the third degree, and are kept in memory in all lodges throughout the world by the ceremonies of the degree.

The other circumstances I would like to mention, may be seen in Richardson's **Monitor of Free-Masonry** (pp.143-145). Here we find that no less than three degrees are said to have originated from the execution of those who violated their obligations. One of the degrees, **Master's Elect of Nine** was founded on the award of punishment to the principal murderer of Hiram Abiff. After that murder was perpetrated, a great assembly of masters was convened to take measures to apprehend the murderers. A stranger came and disclosed the fact that he had discovered a person concealed in a cave near Joppa, who answered the description of one of the supposed murderers. Solomon appointed nine masters to proceed to the spot with the stranger as guide.

On the way, Joabert, one of the nine, learned from the guide the location of the cavern, and he made his way there apart from the rest, where, by the light of a lamp, he discovered the murderer fast asleep, with a poniard at his feet. He took the poniard and stabbed him, first in the head, and then in the heart. The villain exclaimed, "vengeance is taken!" And then expired. Joabert then cut off the murderers head, and taking it in his hand, and the bloody knife in the other, returned to Jerusalem with his companions. Solomon was at first very much offended that Joabert had put it out of his power to take vengeance himself, in presence of, and as a warning to, the rest of the workmen to be faithful to their trust; but by proper intercession was again reconciled. Joabert became highly favored of Solomon, who conferred on him and his eight companions, the title of **Master's Elect of Nine**. The degree of **Master's Elect of Nine**, was founded on this execution. Joabert and his companions were rewarded for their zeal in the work of death, by new and distinguished honors; and a new degree instituted, the emblems and furniture of which are designed to transmit to posterity a representation of the bloody deed. The aprons worn by the brethren of this degree, are white, lined with black, speckled with blood; on the flap a bloody arm with a poniard; on the body of the apron is a bloody arm holding by the hair a bloody head. (see Foldout)

About six months after the execution of the traitor mentioned in the preceding degree of elected knights, more of the traitors were discovered in the country of Cheth. Solomon then elected fifteen masters, in whom he could place the highest confidence, and among whom were those who had been in the cavern, at the execution of the first traitor, and sent them in quest of the villains. They discovered them cutting stone in the quarry; they immediately seized them and bound them in chains. When they arrived at Jerusalem, they were imprisoned in the tower of Achizer, and the next morning a punishment was inflicted on them adequate to their crimes. On this execution is founded the degree of **Master's Elect of Fifteen**. The next degree in the monitor, called **Sublime Knights Elected**, was instituted for the express purpose of honoring and rewarding those who had executed the traitors, and of preparing the way to honor and exalt other worthy assassins from the lower degrees. The history of the degree says, after vengeance had been fully taken on the traitors, Solomon instituted this degree both as a reward for the zeal and integrity of the **Master's Elect of Fifteen**, and also by their promotion to make room for raising other worthy brethren from the lower degrees to that of **Masters Elect of Fifteen**.

These circumstances prove beyond a doubt, that the institution claims authority to take the lives of those who violate their obligations. In ancient times, those who became Masonic traitors by revealing masonry, or by some other offense, were by the authority of the institution, put to death. Have these "ancient landmarks of the order" been removed? Have these "ancient usages and customs" been put away? Every person before he is permitted to enter the Masonic Lodge, "hoodwinked and with a cable-tow around his neck," is made to promise, that he will cheerfully conform to all the ancient established usages and customs of the fraternity. A fellow craft is charged thus -"our laws and regulations you are strenuously to support, and be always ready to **assist in seeing them duly executed**." A master mason is charged thus - "The ancient landmarks of the order, entrusted to your care, you are **carefully to preserve**; and never suffer them to be infringed, nor countenance a deviation from the established usages and customs of the fraternity." Add to this, every member swears to obey all summons, given, handed, sent or thrown to him, from the hand of a brother, or from the body of a just and lawfully constituted lodge, no matter what the command is, or what the summons is. Should a grand master command or summons any number of brethren to apprehend and execute one who had violated his obligations, they are bound, by ancient usages, customs, and laws; by charges, promises, and oaths, to obey.

Now if there is any doubt at all, on the subject of obedience, we will summons one of masonry's most knowledgeable authors, Albert G. Mackey, 33°. In his **Encyclopedia of Freemasonry**, (p. 525) we read - "The doctrine of obedience to constituted authority is strongly inculcated in all the Old Constitutions as necessary to the preservation of the association. In them it is directed that every mason shall prefer his elder and put him to **worship**. The first duty of every mason is to obey the mandate of the master. But if that mandate should have been unlawful or oppressive, he will find his redress in the Grand Lodge, which will review the case and render justice. This spirit of instant obedience and submission to authority constitutes the great safeguard of the institution. Freemasonry more resembles a military than a political organization. The order must at once be obeyed; its character and its consequences may be matters of subsequent inquiry. The Masonic rule of obedience is like the nautical, imperative: Obey orders, even if you break owners."

In Webb's Monitor, (p. 196) he says - "The first duty of the reader of this synopsis is to obey the edicts of his Grand Lodge. Right or wrong, his very existence as a Mason hangs upon obedience to the powers immediately set above him. The one unpardonable crime in a Mason is contumacy (insubordination) or disobedience."

A.T.C. Pierson in **Traditions of Freemasonry** (p. 30) states - "We may not call to question the propriety of this organization, if we would be Masons we must yield private judgement." Or in other words, so far as his Masonic standing is concerned, no member of the fraternity is allowed to exercise his own judgment, but must submit to the decrees of the order, and believe whatever the Masonic ritual teaches. This is Masonic law, inflexible and unchangeable, and beyond this no Mason dare go. He must obey implicitly, whether he likes it or not, and whether the command given, or the statement made be "right or wrong," he "must yield his private judgment," and allow another man, less moral and less intelligent perhaps, to think and judge for him as regards Masonry. And if he refuses to do so, which is very seldom the case, he violates his obligations, and commits "the one unpardonable crime in a Mason."

In **Standard Freemasonry Illustrated**, (pp. 234-236) we read - The initiate swears to "obey all signs and summonses" given or sent by lodges or individuals of any higher degree. This fearful oath subjects him to an unknown multitude of men and lodges throughout the land or world, wherever there are Masons. He is now blindfolded, stripped, badgered, befooled and half demented, or he would stand back with horror at such peril to his person and liberty, exposing himself to demands at all times, by night or day, from persons of whose character and motives he can know nothing but that they, as he has, have been put through the ceremonies and sworn the oaths which he is now going through. Stupefied and bewitched as candidates are at this point, many, it would seem, shrink and hesitate at these horrible obligations, which bind them to "obey summonses" of Jews, Arabs, Mohammedans or Christians, at home or abroad, wherever they may be when the summons reaches them, around the globe!

Albert Mackey in **Mackey's Lexicon**, (p. 185) states that "To its decrees unlimited obedience must be paid by every lodge and every Mason situated within its control," and reminded of the penalties to which he had sworn his consent!

To reconcile the hesitating to such obligations they are told by high Masonic authority (Pierson's Traditions) which has already been quoted, "We may not call in question the propriety of this organization. We must yield private judgment!" And Pierson adds the blasphemy of putting lodge law for the law of God, and quoting, "To the law and to the testimony; if any man walk not according to this rule it is because there is no light in him." This comes as near shameless insolence toward God as human depravity can reach. Hesitating candidates are brought to take these oaths by the combined pressure of various motives; their previous promises to accept and comply with all "customs and regulations" of the order, of which the oath is one; the difficulty of getting out; being stripped, haltered, and completely in the power of the men around them, whom they cannot see; the impression is kept up that the whole thing is a harmless joke; the lying assurance, repeated over and over, that there is nothing in it which conflicts with their duties to God or men; and that they are only following the footsteps of great and good men, and that they will see all right in the end. Under this combined pressure the oath is taken, and the candidate is told he is now the recipient of that particular degree. The man is, thenceforth, not only dechristianized but partially dishumanized. He has no private judgment in religion; that is gone, given up to the lodge. Shame and lurking terror struggle in him for the mastery. His family and Christian brethren, if he has them, are all outside, all "profane!" - and he goes to them like a debauched woman to her husband, who has given herself to another. His heart is hollow. In the lodge he has been told to "pray," and prayers were offered over him where Christ is shut out; and if his bosom was opened as required, "the god of this world" entered to its throne.

And if this experiment has failed to seal the candidate to Satan, the "shock of enlightenment" follows, which Mackey tells us, "is the symbol of the birth of intellectual light" (Ritual p. 34), that is to say, the devil's counterfeit of "the renewing of the Holy Ghost." And if the soul of the poor proselyte gives its assent to what he is passing through, he may already have become in the words of Jesus Christ, "two-fold more the child of hell" than those who are initiating him into that degree of masonry. (Matt. 23:15).

With what confidence can anyone say, that the institution is not bound, and does not consider itself bound, to execute those who willfully violate their obligations? If a doubt still remains in the mind of the reader, it must be removed by the following oath of **Master's Elect of Fifteen**. The candidate swears - "And to be ready to inflict the same penalty (to have the body opened perpendicularly and horizontally, and the head cut off and placed on the highest pinnacle in the world) on all who disclose the secrets of this degree."

Then in the 28th degree of **Knights of the Sun**, we read - "By the man you saw peeping, and who was discovered, and seized and conducted to death, is an emblem of those who come to be initiated into our sacred mysteries through a motive of curiosity; and if so indiscreet as to divulge their obligations, we are bound to cause their DEATH, and to take **vengeance** on the treason by the **destruction** of the traitor."

Is there nothing here which ought to interest and alarm every individual who names the name of Christ. Can professors of Christianity fold their arms and look on with indifference? Can they see their fellow men robbed of their enjoyment, of their equal rights, and of their lives, in strict conformity to the laws of an extensive and powerful society - a society which had its origin in the dark ages of the world, and which now enrolls on its list many of their professed brethren in Christ? I say, can they look upon all this and withhold their influence to bring into disrepute this corrupt institution? Many will reply, it is all speculation; or it is best to be still and say nothing about it. How often are such persons heard to say, "we know nothing about masonry and care nothing about it, and shall use no influence, either to build it up or pull it down!" Their influence, however, is generally made to weigh in favor of the institution; and although they pretend to be ignorant of it, they too often reproach and slander those who, from a fair investigation of the subject, know much about it, and are honestly laboring to inform others. If they know nothing about masonry, isn't it high time they examined it for themselves? Can they be justified in closing their eyes to the light when it shines around them?

Chapter 8

MASONIC SECRECY

Albert Mackey 33°, in **Encyclopedia of Freemasonry** (p. 675), under the heading of SECRECY AND SILENCE says: "These virtues constitute the very essence of all Masonic character; they are the safeguard of the Institution, giving to it all its security and perpetuity (long existence), and are enforced by frequent admonitions in all the degrees, from the lowest to the highest."

Albert Mackey 33°, in **Masonic Jurisprudence** (pp. 17-18), under the heading Landmark Twenty-Third says: "The secrecy of this institution is another and most important landmark...If divested of its secret character, it would lose its identity, and would cease to be Freemasonry...death of the order would follow its legalized exposure. Freemasonry, as a secret association, has lived unchanged for centuries, as an open society it would not last for as many years."

Albert Pike 33°, in **Morals and Dogma** (p. 109), says: "Secrecy is indispensable in a Mason of whatever Degree. It is the first and almost the only lesson taught to the Entered Apprentice."

Speaking of the Entered Apprentice, all of my Masonic rituals and monitors show the candidate hoodwinked and half naked, kneeling at a Masonic altar with a rope around his neck, swearing not to make known that which a Masonic publishing company prints and sells to any one who has the money and request it.

Daniel Sickels 33°, in **Ahiman Rezon** (p. 61), says: "One of the most notable features of Freemasonry - one, certainly which attracts, more than any thing else, the attention of the profane world - is that veil of mystery - that awful secrecy - behind which it moves and acts. From the earliest periods, this has invariably been a distinctive characteristic of the institution; and today, as of old, the first obligation of a mason - his supreme duty - is that of silence and secrecy."

Apparently Masonry as a business is not bound by what it makes its dupes swear to. I am not a mason, and never intend to be one, yet I have purchased some of the most secret items in the Masonic Lodge, including all of the oaths and obligations from the First Degree thru the Thirty-Third Degree. Some of the items range from a few dollars in price to several hundred, depending on what you want. See invoices at the back of this chapter.

Thomas S. Webb, in **Webb's Monitor** (p. 42) says: "Fortitude is that noble and steady purpose of the mind, whereby we are enabled to undergo any pain, peril or danger, when prudently deemed expedient. This virtue is equally distant from rashness and cowardice; and, like the former, should be deeply impressed upon the mind of every mason, as a safeguard or security against any illegal attack that may be made, by force or otherwise, to extort from him any of those secrets with which he has been so solemnly entrusted; and which was emblematically represented upon his first admission into the lodge."

This would really be funny if it were not so serious. Why should I attack a poor mason, and spend hours forcing him to talk and reveal his silly little secrets, when, as I have said before, I can purchase them for just a few dollars. Let us continue now with the same author and the same book (p. 257). Charge to a new made Intimate Secretary: "My brother, I receive you an Intimate secretary, on your promise to be faithful to the order in which you have just now entered. We hope, brother, that your fidelity will be proof to every trial; and that this sword, with which we arm you, will defend you from the attacks of those, who may try to extort from you those secrets which we are now about to confer upon you."

Isn't this ridiculous? Masons have such a complex, when it comes to their precious secrets, that they must carry a sword in defence of all those who would attack them, and extort their secrets from them. How many times in the last ten years have you read in the Middletown Journal, or seen on the local news, where some poor, unsuspecting mason was kidnapped and brutally beaten for not revealing the secrets of the lodge?

William J. Whalen, in **Christianity and American Freemasonry** (p. 98), says: "Actually, what the Masonic candidates swear to conceal is nothing more than a few passwords, secret grips, and lodge rites. Masonry may be entitled to preserve harmless secrets in order to heighten the interest of prospective members and amuse the brethren. It may employ passwords to exclude the merely curious from its assemblies. But to suggest that the oaths demanded of the candidate are needed to protect such secrets is ridiculous. A gentlemen's promise would serve as well.

A family may keep certain secrets within the family circle, but can we imagine the father gathering his children around the family altar, blindfolding them, and asking them to place their hands on the Holy Bible and to declare that they would have their toes split one by one, their hair pulled out by the roots, and their legs tied in a bow knot rather than reveal that the front door key is usually kept under the doormat"?

If Masonry is such a wonderful institution, if it is that which is most needed in this present age, if it is doing the work of the church, and a hand-maid of Christianity, then why impose such terrible oaths, and bind the candidate under such horrible death penalties to keep it a secret? Mr. Carl H. Claudy, Masonic author, answers that for us when he says: "Men are men the world over. That which is hidden is sought; that which is forbidden is desired; that which is secret is studied; that which is held rare is held valuable. Every Mason knows that the privacy of the Masonic ceremonies lends dignity to them and make them most impressive."

Speaking of dignity, I would like to ask Mr. Claudy what he thinks of the initiation for the Shriners? Would he say for example, that pretending that a dog is pissing in the initiate's face is lending dignity to the ceremony and making it more impressive; doesn't that sound like a real solemn occasion? You can read this for yourself under Initiation, on pages 25-26 of **"The Ancient Arabic Order Nobles of the Mystic Shrine"** published by the Ezra A. Cook Publishing Co. Inc., Chicago, Ill.

I would like to end this chapter with a statement I copied from my Masonic Scrapbook, and again I failed to write down the author's name, because I never planned to use it in a book. He says: "In an age where an optical fiber in your T.V. watches you while you watch it, and a transmitter is easily capped over in the cavity of a tooth, and a spy satellite takes a picture from eight miles up and you can read a license plate number, you have got to be pretty gullible to believe that anything is really secret. Stands to reason though, if a man will allow himself to be blindfolded and a cable-tow put around his neck, and led away like a goat, the odds are he will believe just about anything."

On the following pages you will find invoices addressed to me from two Masonic Supply Companies from which I purchased aprons, skulls, cordons, books, certificates, pictures, signet rings, name plates, auto emblems, Masonic I.D. cards, etc., etc.

- PRINTING-BINDING
- OFFICE SUPPLIES-FURNITURE
- UNIFORMS-REGALIA
- FRATERNAL SUPPLIES

IHLING BROS. EVERARD CO. 2022 Fulford, Kalamazoo, Michigan 49001-4090, Phone 616-381-1340

December 9, 1988

Mr. Elmer Garitson
401 Baltimore Street
Middletown, OH 45044

Dear Mr. Garitson:

I'm writing for two reasons: One, to acknwledge the receipt of your check in the amount of $330.00 for those Scottish Rite items needed. We are in the process of processing this order right now, and I will be responding to you shortly with your many questions in that note.

The purpose of this letter is to quote to you the 15° girdle #9858 Southern Jurisdiction. It is priced as follows: In bonaz embroidery - $309.55. In Swiss embroidery - $399.75. This price is subject to insured delivery and handling charges. Please allow ample time for delivery.

Thank you for coming to Ihling Bros.

Sincerely and fraternally,

IHLING BROS. EVERARD CO.

Gerry E. Millar,
Sales Representative

GEM:ln

TOLL FREE [illegible]
1-800-[illegible]-4232

SERVING YOU SINCE 1869

- PRINTING - BINDING
- OFFICE SUPPLIES - FURNITURE
- UNIFORMS - REGALIA
- FRATERNAL SUPPLIES

IHLING BROS. EVERARD CO. 2022 Fulford, Kalamazoo, Michigan 49001-4090, Phone 616 - 381-1340

December 19, 1988

Mr. Elmer Garitson
401 Baltimore Street
Middletown, OH 45044

Dear Mr. Garitson:

By this time you should have received your sale acknowledgement for the 9° apron, 10° cordon and the signet ring.

Also, in your letter, you asked several questions. They are first, the 15° apron. Yes, it is the same price as listed on your price list under the Swiss column.

Second, you requested a 1989 Masonic Catalog which you will find enclosed.

Third, concerning the decapitated head, no, it is not available.

Fourth, concerning the genuine skull, the information I gave you over the phone has now been changed. The genuine skull is no longer available. The skull you can receive now is plastic and sells for $288.45. It is the same skull that is used in the Knights Templar and will have the cut top and gold leaf lining. If you desire you want a plastic skull and do not want it with a cut top and gold leaf lining, we will see what we can do about purchasing one without the cut top and lining. We will do our best for you. The current price is $288.45.

Last of all you asked about the dagger for the 9°. It is silver and gold plated. This is the reason for the price.

Thank you for coming to Ihling Bros. We certainly do appreciate it.

Sincerely and fraternally,

IHLING BROS. EVERARD CO.

Gerry E. Millar,
Sales Representative

TOLL FREE NUMBER
1-800-999-4232

GEM:ln

Enclosure

SERVING YOU SINCE 1869

INVOICE

IHLING BROS. EVERARD CO.

2022 FULFORD ST. • KALAMAZOO, MICHIGAN 49001-4090 • PHONE (616) 381-1340

DATE ENT. 12-9-88

PRINTING, BINDING, BLANK BOOKS
STATIONERY, OFFICE SUPPLIES
FURNITURE

SECRET SOCIETY REGALIA
COSTUMES AND SUPPLIES
UNIFORMS

SOLD TO

Elmer Garitson
401 Baltimore St.
Middletown, OH 45044

SHIPPED VIA US MAIL 1ST CL.
SALESMAN Millar
TERMS CWO 330.00

SALE NO. K-57475
PLEASE DETACH AND RETURN THIS PORTION WITH PAYMENT
YOUR NO.

DATE SHIPPED 2-01-89

3918	1	9° Apron, Southern Jurisdiction swiss embroidery, white lambskin, black lining and border, drops of blood to be red, emblems in appropriate colors.		156.55
	1	Cordon, lined, shaped to fit closely at neck and over shoulder, face of black satin black satin with three swiss embroidered heads, fetted with fastner for jewel, worn from right to left		131.30
A3310000	1	Southern Jurisdiction Signet Ring, size 11½		36.10
				323.95
		THANK YOU FOR YOUR ORDER.		
		Your remittance has been Credited as follows:		
		Total amount of Invoice........ 332.43		
		Remittance received with your order 330.00		
		BALANCE DUE TO → 2.43		
		IHLING BROS. EVERARD CO.		
		INSURED DELIVERY & HANDLING		8.48
		IHLING BROS. EVERARD CO. KALAMAZOO, MICHIGAN	TOTAL	332.43

- PRINTING - BINDING
- OFFICE SUPPLIES - FURNITURE
- UNIFORMS - REGALIA
- FRATERNAL SUPPLIES

IHLING BROS. EVERARD CO. 2022 Fulford, Kalamazoo, Michigan 49001-4090, Phone 616-381-1340

January 10, 1989

Mr. Elmer Garitson
401 Baltimore Street
Middletown, OH 45044

Dear Mr. Garitson:

Thank you for your recent order for the plastic skull and 9° jewel. You will find the acknowledgement enclosed.

Also, in response to our conversation concerning a Scottish Rite Catalog, we do not have one specifically made up for Scottish Rite. What I have sent you is all the information that we have. For those items that you are in need of, just get in contact with us. We will then update and send you current information.

We certainly do appreciate the business you have been sending to Ihling Bros. and we look forward to continuing to serve you and your Scottish Rite brothers during the coming months.

Sincerely and fraternally,

IHLING BROS. EVERARD CO.

Gerry E. Millar,
Sales Representative

GEM:ln

Enclosures

SERVING YOU SINCE 1869

ACKNOWLEDGEMENT

IHLING BROS. EVERARD CO.

2022 FULFORD ST. • KALAMAZOO, MICHIGAN 49001-4090 • PHONE (616) 381-1340
TOLL FREE 800-828-3662 (MICHIGAN 616-381-1340 COLLECT)

PRINTING, BINDING, BLANK BOOKS
STATIONERY, OFFICE SUPPLIES
FURNITURE

SECRET SOCIETY REGALIA
COSTUMES AND SUPPLIES
UNIFORMS

THIS ACKNOWLEDGES YOUR ORDER

Thank you. We have placed your order in turn for shipment promptly as we can complete it. IT DOES NOT indicate goods have been shipped.

If this acknowledgment does not represent your entire order, do not be alarmed. Our aim is to ship Stock Items within 48 hours, consequently acknowledgment is not sent for such items.

DO NOT REMIT until you receive final and complete figures including postage if prepaid.

DATE ENT. 1-5-89

SOLD TO

Elmer Garitson
401 Baltimore St.
Middletown, OH 45044

SHIPPED VIA

SALESMAN MA

TERMS CWO 375.00

SALE NO. K -58186

YOUR NO.

M422086	1	Plastic Skull, cut top, gold leaf lining	288.45
132823	1	9° AASR Jewel, (dagger), gold & silver plate, size 4½"	78.60
			367.05

ACKNOWLEDGEMENT
ORDER CONFIRMATION DO NOT PAY

ORDER CONFIRMATION
DO NOT PAY

INSURED DELIVERY & HANDLING

ORDER CONFIRMATION
DO NOT PAY

INVOICE

IHLING BROS. EVERARD CO.

2022 FULFORD ST. • KALAMAZOO, MICHIGAN 49001-4090 • PHONE (616) 381-1340

DATE ENT. 2-7-89

PRINTING, BINDING, BLANK BOOKS
STATIONERY, OFFICE SUPPLIES
FURNITURE

SECRET SOCIETY REGALIA
COSTUMES AND SUPPLIES
UNIFORMS

SOLD TO
Elmer Garitson
401 Baltimore St.
Middletown, OH 45044

SHIPPED VIA UPS overnight Express mail
SALESMAN Millar
TERMS CWO 399.75
SALE NO. K-59406
PLEASE DETACH AND RETURN THIS PORTION WITH PAYMENT
YOUR NO.
DATE SHIPPED 3-20-89

9859 rected	1	Girdle or Waist sash, 15° white moire satin, lined, reinforced to hold shape, Top and Bottom of 4" sash is bordered in #3598-½" wide gold braid, 2" fringe along bottom is gold twist Embroidery is swiss in colors, Size to be adjustable 10" starting at 36" and going to 46" by use of concealed snaps. The drape should look like photostat and be bordered in #3598-½" wide gold braid, bottom of drape is 6" wide tapering to simulated Bow, same fringe as on sash is on bottom of bow and drape, fasten bow & drape to sash permanetly on one end, adjustment to be behind bow & drape NO jewel to be suspended from sash.	THANK YOU FOR YOUR ORDER. Your remittance has been Credited as follows:	399.75 Total amount of Invoice 412.75 Remittance received with your order 399.75 BALANCE DUE 13.00 IHLING BROS. EVERARD CO.
		INSURED DELIVERY & HANDLING		13.00
		IHLING BROS. EVERARD CO. KALAMAZOO, MICHIGAN	TOTAL	412.75

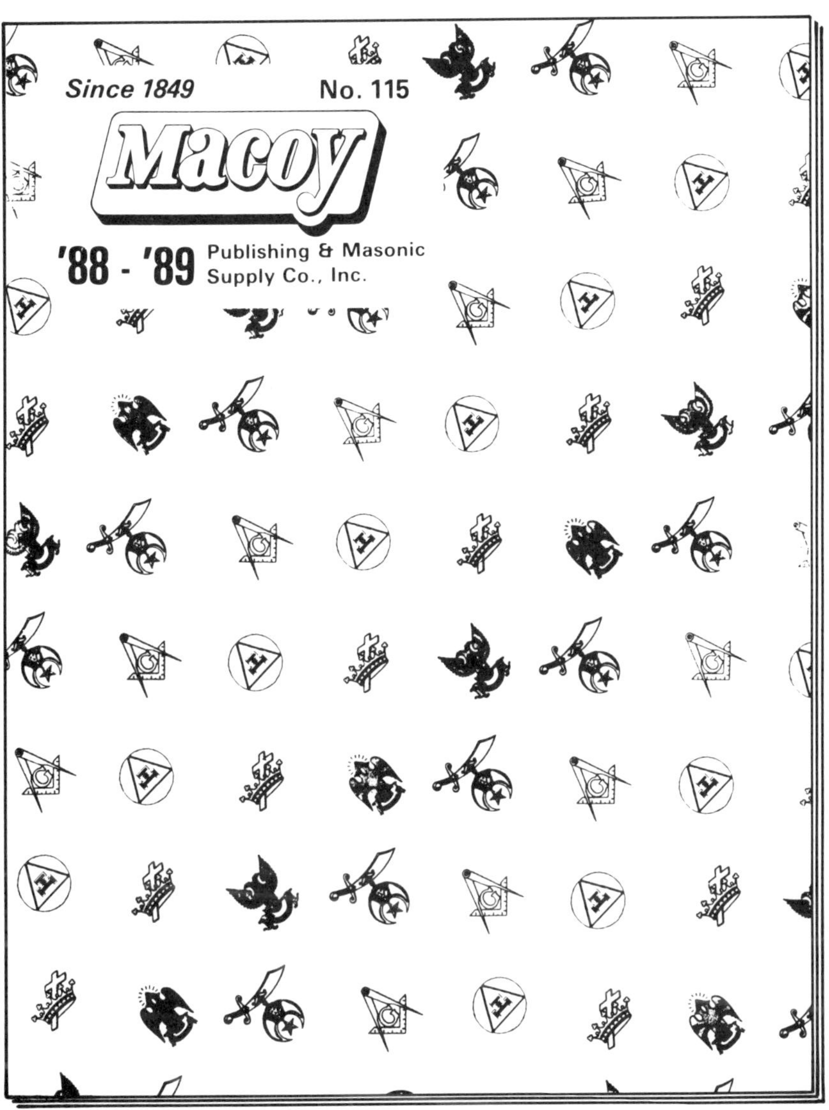
Since 1849
No. 115
Macoy
'88 - '89
Publishing & Masonic
Supply Co., Inc.

INVOICE

CUSTOMER'S COPY

Macoy

P.O. Box 9759
Richmond, Virginia 23228-0759
Phone: (804) 262-6551

CUSTOMER NUMBER
0HIA08

SHIP TO

SOLD TO

ELMER GARITSON
401 BALTIMORE ST
MIDDLETOWN
OH 45044

DATE	INVOICE NO.
11-14-88	256308

TERMS: NET 30

MACOY ORDER NO.	ORDER DATE	SHIP DATE	VIA:	
51371C	11-09-88	11-11-88	COD-125.00	2

ORDER	SHP'D.	B. ORD.	ITEM NUMBER	UNIT	DESCRIPTION	LIST PRICE		AMOUNT
9999	0	0			RC'D 125.00	.000		.00
1	1	0	1106	EA	WASHINGTON AS WM	7.500		7.50
1	1	0	1105	EA	STEPS OF FREEMASONRY	3.500		3.50
1	1	0	1114	EA	DARKNESS TO LIGHT	5.000		5.00
1	1	0	1107	EA	11X14 LORD'S PRAYER	3.000		3.00
1	1	0	1116/K	EA	THE MASONIC CHART	3.000		3.00
1	1	0	1565/SC	EA	S & C EMBR EMB 3' GD/GR/R	2.500		2.50
1	1	0	8197/M	EA	MASONIC KEY CHAIN	2.500		2.50
2	2	0	8054	EA	MASONIC POCKET PIECE	1.500		3.00
1	1	0	8056	EA	BRONZE POCKET PIECE	7.500		7.50
1	1	0	1240	EA	RAM POCKET PIECE	2.250		2.25
2	2	0	9000	EA	LAMBSKIN MAT	1.250		2.50
1	1	0	8429	EA	MASONIC PLAQUE	1.750		1.75
1	0	1	8074	EA	STRUCTURE OF FREEMASONRY	9.500		.00
1	1	0	8081	EA	WHAT IS A MASON PLAQUE	9.000		9.00
50	50	0	8081/F	EA	"WHAT IS A MASON?" CARD	.100	50.00	2.50
1	1	0	9570	PKG	(36)MAS 3/4"GOLD STICKERS	1.000		1.00
1	1	0	9571	PKG	(35)OES 3/4"GOLD STICKERS	1.000		1.00
1	1	0	8020	EA	MINIATURE WOODEN GAVEL	2.000		2.00

K

NON TAX MDSE.	TAXABLE MDSE.	SALES TAX	PACKING & SHIPPING	INSURANCE & MISCS.	INVOICE TOTAL ➡	

The obligation in this degree is now given to the candidate in the usual form. While candidate is taking it, kneeling at the altar, the companions all stand over him with raised poniards, as if about to stab him. Meantime the bloody head is standing on the altar, facing him with ghastly grin.

The obligation is as follows:—

I do solemnly swear, in the presence of Almighty God, that I will revenge the assassination of our worthy Master, Hiram Abiff, not only on the murderers, but also on all who may betray the secrets of this degree; and furthermore, that I will keep and protect this Order with all my might, and the brethren, in general, with all my power, and furthermore, that I will obey the decrees of the Grand Council of Princes of Jerusalem; and, if I violate this, my obligation, I consent to be struck with the dreadful poniard of vengeance, now presented to me, and to have my head cut off, and stuck on the highest pole, or pinnacle, in the eastern part of the world, as a monument of my villany! Amen! amen! amen! amen!

Master's Elect Of Nine

IHLING BROS. EVERARD CO.

2022 FULFORD STREET / KALAMAZOO, MICHIGAN 49001-4090

CATALOG M
1989

Past Grand Master Apron — Grand Lodge of Japan F. & A. M.

embroidered in our Kalamazoo factory

MASONIC

REGALIA AND SUPPLIES

BLUE LODGE • CHAPTER • COUNCIL • COMMANDERY

TOLL FREE PHONE: 800/999-4232

Catalog from which I purchased some of Masonry's most "Secret" items, such as skull, apron, sash and cordon, used in the degrees of vengeance.

You promised, when you entered the chamber of reflection, that you would conform to all the ceremonies, rules, and regulations of this Encampment. We have your promise in writing. We expect you will proceed. All Sir Knights who have taken this degree, have participated in the fifth libation; and if there is anything in it that you do not perfectly understand, it will be qualified and explained to your satisfaction.

Candidate takes the skull in his hand, and repeats after the Grand Commander as follows: This pure wine, I take from this cup, in testimony of my belief of the mortality of the body and the immortality of the soul; and as the sins of the whole world were laid upon the head of our Saviour, so may the sins of the person whose skull this once was, be heaped upon my head, in addition to my own; and may they appear in judgement against me, both here and hereafter, should I violate or transgress any obligation in Masonry, or the Orders of Knighthood which I have heretofore taken, take at this time, or may hereafter be instructed in. So help me God. [Drinks of the wine.]

Grand Commander (taking skull from candidate)—This is called the sealed obligation, because any promise of secrecy, made in reference to this obligation, is considered by Knights Templars to be more binding than any other obligation can be.

The Sealed Obligation

Chapter 9

MASONIC DOCTRINE VERSES THE BIBLE

The mysteries of masonry are solemnly concealed from the world; but the mysteries of godliness are revealed, and ministers are employed by our saviour, for the express purpose of making these mysteries known to all men. "To make all men see," says Paul, "what is the fellowship of the mystery, which from the beginning of the world hath been hid in God;" not in a Masonic lodge.

JESUS CHRIST

Ministers and Christians are in possession of no mysteries from God, which they are to conceal from any of their fellow creatures. They are to communicate to the world all the information they can, relative to the word which was with God, and was God, and was made flesh and dwelt among us.

Masonry does not look upon Jesus Christ as the Savior of the world, but rather teaches that He was just one of many great reformers and moralists.

Manly P. Hall 33°, in **The Lost Keys of Freemasonry**, (p. 65) says: "Christ, Buddha or Mohammed, the name means little, for he (the mason) recognizes only the light and not the bearer."

Someone has made the statement, and I must say that I agree, that, "all worship and acknowledgment paid to any god apart from Jesus Christ is idolatry."

W. L. Wilmshurst, in **The Meaning of Masonry**, (p. 105) says: "Our science in its universality limits our conception to no one exemplar. Take the nearest and most familiar to you, the one under whose protection you were racially born, and who therefore may serve you best; for each is able to bring you to the center, though each may have his separate method."

In other words Mr. Wilmshurst is telling us, that whatever country or nation we are from, we should choose that exemplar to follow, whether it be Christ, Buddha, or Mohammed, because each one can get us to heaven, though they all have separate methods of doing so.

Albert Pike 33°, in **Morals and Dogma**, (p. 525) states: "It (Masonry) reverences all the great reformers. It sees in Moses, the Lawgiver of the Jews, in Confucius and Zoraster, in Jesus of Nazareth, and in the Arabian Iconoclast, great teachers of morality, and eminent reformers, if no more: and allows every brother of the Order to assign to each such higher and even divine character as his creed and truth require."

In effect then, Masonry says, "If you want to deem Jesus of Nazareth divine and wish to worship Him, that is fine. If you believe Zoraster was divine, that's fine too, whomever you deem divine and worship is your business. As for Masonry, we believe they are all great moralists."

Is this what the bible teaches? Matt.17:5 - *"This is my beloved Son, in whom I am well pleased; hear ye him."* John 14:6 - *"Jesus saith unto him, I am the way, the truth, and the life: no man cometh unto the Father, but by me."* Acts 4:12 - *"Neither is there salvation in any other, for there is none other name under heaven given among men, whereby ye must be saved,"* and then 1 Tim. 2:5 - *"For there is one God, and one mediator between God and men, the man Christ Jesus."*

Albert Pike 33°, in **Morals and Dogma**, (p. 308) says: "No one Mason has the right to measure for another, within the walls of a Masonic Temple, the degree of veneration which he shall feel for any Reformer, or the Founder of any Religion."

Mrs. E. M. Storms, in her book entitled, **Should a Christian Be a Mason**, (p. 37) says, concerning the above statement by Pike: "Strange law for a temple of supposedly 'Christian' teachings whose God is reported by Christians to be Christ! This tactic, of course, clears the path for

Masonry to teach its own mishmash of Christian and Kabbalistic doctrine without any rebuttal from its initiates. It also closes the door for any Christian Mason to witness for Jesus Christ, or point other masons to saving faith through His shed blood."

Manly P. Hall 33°, in **Lost Keys of Freemasonry**, (pp. 15 & 22) says: "A religion is a divinely inspired code of morals. A religious person is one inspired to nobler living by this code. He is identified by the code which is his source of illumation. Thus we may say that a Christian is one who receives his spiritual ideals of right and wrong from the message of the Christ, while a Buddhist is one who molds his life into the archetype of morality given by the great Gautama, or one of the other Buddhas.

Most of the religions of the world are like processions: one leads, and the many follow. The Christian follows the gentle Nazarene up the winding slopes of Calvary. The Buddhist follows his great emancipator through his wanderings in the wilderness. The Mohammedan makes his pilgrimage across the desert sands to the black tent at Mecca. Truth leads, and ignorance follows in his train."

J. D. Buck in **Mystic Masonry** (pp. 62-63) says: "It is far more important that men should strive to become Christs than that they should believe that Jesus was Christ. Jesus is no less Divine because all men may reach the same Divine perfection.

It has also been shown that every act in the drama of the life of Jesus, and every quality assigned to Christ, is to be found in the life of Krishna and in the legend of all the Sun-Gods from the remotest antiquity.

That which the orthodox Christian will find to oppose to this view is, not that it dethrones or degrades Christ, but that it disproves the idea of Christ as their exclusive possession, and denies that all other religions are less Divine than their own."

R. Swinburne Clymer, in **Mysticism of Masonry**, (p. 47) says: "In defying Jesus, the whole of humanity is bereft of Christos as an eternal potency within every human soul. In thus deifying one man, they have orphaned the whole of humanity, and at the same time built a false and destructive scheme of salvation. Few candidates may be aware that Hiram, whom they have represented and personified, is ideally and precisely the same as Jesus."

From the remarks in this chapter, we may infer, that masonry in the assumed character of religion, is a dangerous system; and will undoubtedly be the means of deceiving many. We are told by Masonic writers, in the most unequivocal terms, that masonry possesses the same excellencies with Christianity, and if they practice the duties of masonry they will be saved. It is easy to make the credulous part of the community believe this, especially when taught by men of influence, and exhibited in the most alluring forms. No doubt there are many of the fraternity who do believe it, and rest their hopes for heaven on masonry. Such men are deceived; and if they die in their deception they will be lost; and their loss can be attributed to the wicked influence of masonry. In consequence of this self-righteous scheme, they have rejected the doctrines of the bible, and built their hopes on the sand.

Masonry is so pleasing to the natural man, that he is easily captivated by it. Christianity demands of him, repentance for his sins, faith in our Lord Jesus Christ, a humble reliance on his vicarious sufferings for salvation, and a persevering practice of the self-denying duties of the cross. For these things he has no relish; his mind is at war with them.

Masonry makes none of these dictatorial demands: it charms him, in every way pleases him; it teaches him, that to practice external morality, will render him virtuous and lovely in the sight of his Maker, and entitle him to a seat in heaven. Read the writings of masons; what do they extol above every thing else? What do they urge upon their members by all that is solemn? The practice of outside religion - "you agree to be a good man and true, and strictly to obey the moral law."

In all the Masonic writings I have read, I never found one instance in which faith and repentance are urged as Masonic duties, or the righteousness of Christ so much as named as the foundation of justification before God. It is self, and is the language of a pharisee who is boasting of heaven with nothing but an outside show, which in his own view renders him "worthy and great." How different is this from the language of a saint; -"O wretched man that I am; who am less than the least of all saints."

The Saviour taught his disciples to pray in his name; and in his name they do pray. A prayer which is not offered in his name is not of faith, is not dictated by the Holy Spirit, is not heard and answered, and is not the prayer of a renewed heart. Masons do not approach God in his name, nor acknowledge it as the medium of communication. I have read dozens of Masonic prayers, in the various monitors and books of instruction, and found not one which was offered in the name of Christ.. The Holy Spirit was not once named. No sins were confessed. What are these, but the prayers of deists? Let me close this topic with the following thought and scripture: Men who offer such prayers are hoping for heaven- Job 27:8 - *"For what is the hope of the hypocrite, though he hath gained, when God taketh away his soul?"*

GOD

Masonry as a professed moral institution, does not acknowledge the true God. It is like the Pantheon at Rome, which acknowledged all the gods of the heathens. Among Mahometans, it acknowledges the god of Mahomet; among pagans, it acknowledges the multiplied gods of pagans. Can it at the same time acknowledge the true God? An institution which acknowledges the true God, acknowledges no other. A Mahometan or a pagan, who is a mason, cannot be excluded from any of the privileges of the order, by those who profess to acknowledge the true God, merely because he does not acknowledge the same. Men of all nations, of all religions, and with their different gods, meet upon this system and hail each other as brethren. Let us now look at masonry's teaching about God:

Carl Claudy, in **Introduction to Freemasonry** (pp. 109-110) says: "One can no more keep secret the idea that God is the very warp and woof of Freemasonry than that He is the essence of all life. The petitioner must declare his faith in a Supreme Being before he may be initiated. But note that he is not required to say, then or ever, what God. He may name Him as he will, Freemasonry cares not. Freemasonry's own especial name for Deity is Great Architect of the Universe. But God, Great Architect of the Universe, Grand Artificer, Grand Master of the Grand Lodge Above, Jehovah, Allah, Buddha, Brahma, Vishnu, Shiva, or Great Geometer, a symbol of the conception shines in the East of every American Masonic Lodge." Then on page 38 of the same book, Mr. Claudy says, "A hundred paths may wind upward around a mountain; at the top they meet".

In the New Age, January 1943, (p. 33) we read: "Masonry's followers are found alike among Christians, Jews, Brahmans, and Turks, for it is the universal decree that:

The one Great God looked down and smiled
And counted each his loving child,
For Turk and Brahman, Monk and Jew,
HAD REACHED HIM THRU THE GOD HE KNEW"

This sounds great for those who teach the Brotherhood of man, and the Fatherhood of God, but in the light of the following scripture, it doesn't mean a thing: John 14:6 - *"no man cometh unto the Father, but by me"*.

Albert Pike 33° in **Morals and Dogma**, (p. 296) says: "The God of nineteen-twentieths of the Christian world is only Bel, Moloch, Zeus, or at best Osiris, Mithras, or Adonai, under another name, worshiped with the old pagan ceremonies and ritualistic formulas. It is the statue of Olympian Jove, worshiped as the Father, in the Christian church that was a pagan temple; it is the statue of Venus, become the Virgin Mary."

Albert Pike equates the Christian God with the heathen abominations.

Listen to another Masonic author by the name of Godfrey Higgins: "Be assured," he says, "that God is equally present with the pious Hindoo in the temple, the Jew in the synagogue, the Mohammedan in the mosque, and the Christian in the church."

By the above statement we can readily see that Godfrey Higgins is totally ignorant of the Word of God, as is most masons. John 3:36 - *"He that believeth on the Son hath everlasting life: and he that believeth not the Son shall not see life; but the wrath of God abideth on him."*

Now, according to the above scripture, where does this leave the Hindoo, the Jew, the Mohammedan, the Jehovah's Witness and every other Christ rejecting false religion and cult? According to John, God is not present with the pious Hindoo, Jew, or Mohammedan, but rather his "wrath abideth on them".

The Masonic teaching on God when summarized, is as follows: There exists but one God. Therefore all of these various religions are worshipping the same God, but under a different name. To them this argument is convincing and conclusive.

But, if what masonry teaches is true, that Baal and Jehovah are the same God, but worshipped under different names, then why did Elijah slay the four hundred prophets of Baal at the brook? Also if Baal was God, why didn't he intervene on behalf of his prophets and prevent all that blood-shed? If these two Gods are the same - why did Jehovah tell Gideon to take his father's young bullock and throw down the altar of Baal and cut down the grove that was by it? Jesus said in Matt. 12:26 - *"And if Satan cast out Satan he is divided against himself; how shall then his kingdom stand?* Would this reasoning not also apply if God were divided?

THE BIBLE

We often see Freemasonry making a big show of the Bible, just as the Pharisees did in relation to their prayers and almsgiving, having it carried in such a manner as to attract attention in all its outdoor processions, as a way of advertising itself in the public's eye; but as a system of religious philosophy, and behind the secret recesses of the Lodge door, we also find that it degrades and mutilates that Bible, despises and ignores its precepts, falsifies its teachings, and dishonors its Divine Author.

The manner in which masons have mutilated the holy scriptures, betrays a want of reverence to Almighty God. Rev. 22:19 - *"And if any man shall take away from the words of the book of this prophecy, God shall take away his part from the tree of life, and out of the holy city, which are written in this book."*

I will show these Masonic mutilations, side by side with the word of God, that the reader may be able to see and compare them for himself.

MASONRY	GOD'S WORD
Charge to be read at opening the lodge. "Wherefore, brethren, lay aside all malice, and guile, and hypocrisies, and envies, and all evil speaking.	Wherefore laying aside all malice, and all guile, and hypocrisies, and envies and all evil speaking. 2. As new-born babes, desire the sincere milk of the word, that ye may grow thereby: 3. If so be ye have tasted that the Lord is gracious.

"If so be, ye have tasted that the Lord is gracious, to whom, coming as unto a living stone, disallowed, indeed, of men, but chosen of God, and precious; ye also, as living stones be ye built up a spiritual house, an holy priesthood, to offer up sacrifices acceptable to God."

4. To whom coming, as unto a living stone, disallowed indeed of men, but chosen of God, and precious.

5. Ye also, as living stones, are built up a spiritual house, an holy priesthood, to offer up spiritual sacrifices, acceptable to God **BY JESUS CHRIST**." 1 Pet. 2:1-5

The charge just quoted is taken from the fourth degree of the York Rite, which is the Mark Master Degree. The scripture used is 1 Peter 2:1-5, and the name Jesus Christ is left out of the fifth verse entirely. I could almost except this as an oversight or a mistake in just one book; but I have before me ten different Masonic manuals, guides, and rituals, by nine different authors over a period of seventy-five years, and every one of them quote the same scripture, for the same degree of masonry, and all nine authors leave out the name of our Lord Jesus Christ in the fifth verse. This has to be more than a coincidence. Below is a listing of the ten books, with their authors, and the page number on which the mutilation appears:

The Masonic Manual	Robert Macoy	86
True Masonic Guide	Robert Macoy	79-80
Monitor of Freemasonry	Jabez Richardson	42-43
Ritual of Freemasonry	Wm. Reeves	68
Craftsman & Freemasons Guide	Cornelius Moore	87-88

Freemasonry Illustrated	Jacob O. Doesburg	364-365
Duncan's Ritual	Malcolm Duncan	156-157
Chapter Degrees	Edmond Ronayne	13
Freemason's Monitor	Thomas Smith Webb	76
Guide To The Royal Arch Chapter	James L. Gould	52

The next example of Bible mutilation by the Masonic lodge, is taken from the opening charge of the seventh degree of the York Rite, known as the Royal Arch Degree. The scripture used is 2 Thess. 3:6, 12 and the Lord Jesus Christ is left out of the sixth verse and the twelfth verse. Another coincidence I suppose. Also I might mention that the York Rite is supposed to be the "Christian" branch of Freemasonry.

MASONRY	GOD'S WORD
The following charge is read at the opening of a chapter. "Now we command you, brethren, that ye withdraw yourself from every brother that walketh disorderly, and not after the tradition which he received of us."	6. Now we commend you, brethren, **IN THE NAME OF OUR LORD JESUS CHRIST,** that ye withdraw yourselves from every brother that walketh disorderly, and not after the tradition which he received of us.
"Now them that are such, we command and exhort, that with quietness they work, and eat their own bread."	12. Now them that are such we command and exhort **BY OUR LORD JESUS CHRIST** that with quietness they work and eat their own bread. 2 Thess. 3:6, 12

The above mutilations of the Bible, are shown exactly alike, in eight different Masonic books, by seven different authors, and are listed hereafter by book, author, and page number on which the mutilation appears, that the reader might be able to compare them as before.

Freemason's Monitor	Thomas Smith Webb	132
Guide To The Royal Arch Chapter	James L. Gould	139-140
Chapter Degrees	Edmond Ronayne	198
Freemasonry Illustrated	Jacob O. Doesburg	499
Craftsman & Freemason's Guide	Cornelius Moore	152
True Masonic Guide	Robert Macoy	146
Ritual of Freemasonry	Wm. Reeves	109
The Masonic Manual	Robert Macoy	157

These alterations of God's Word cannot be a mistake; the design is too visible. It was the intention of masons not to give those passages of scripture as they are found in the Bible. How shall we account for this? How inconsistent with the pretensions of the institution! After all the things masons have said about the moral excellence of their system, it is evident that the very name of "our Lord Jesus Christ" is disgusting to them; or they would not erase it from the scriptures that they quote.

Are they at liberty to treat God's Word in this manner? If they may handle a few passages in this way, they may the whole bible. What kind of a bible would we have if it were to come through the hands of masons? It would be vastly different from what it is now. It would be like their religion, designed to please all men, even "men of the most opposite tenets, and of the most contradictory opinions." From this irreverent manner of using the scriptures, it is evident, masons regard them no more than any uninspired book;

and the plain reading of them is unfavorable to their religion. Should the bible receive this kind of treatment from professed infidels, it would not be so unaccountable.

Maybe these good masons have never read in the book of Jeremiah the account of God's judgment upon Jehoiakim, king of Judah, for the mutilation of His Word. Jer. 36:22-24 - *"Now the king sat in the winterhouse in the ninth month: and there was a fire on the hearth burning before him. And it came to pass, that when Jehudi had read three or four leaves, he cut it with a penknife, and cast it into the fire that was on the hearth, until all the roll was consumed in the fire that was on the hearth. Yet they were not afraid, nor rent their garments, neither the king, nor any of his servants that heard all these words."* Could it be that there is no fear of God amongst the Lodge?

This willful mutilation of the bible and the rejection of Jesus Christ as Lord is an unvarying principle in masonry, and every candidate, minister, or Sunday school teacher, is solemnly sworn under a death penalty to "ever maintain and support" this God-dishonoring principle. Thus rejecting Jesus Christ masonry rejects the true God - and for this reason it is a damning delusion for masons to make their boast of "trust in God," while they knowingly repudiate and dishonor Him. How can Freemasons expect to live with Jesus in heaven, when they so irreverently reject and black ball Him from their lodges on earth?

I guess this isn't too difficult to understand though, when we consider what Masonic authors and teachers have to say concerning the bible. FIRST - Masonry teaches that the bible is only a symbol of the will of God, and that it is not divine or inspired.

Henry W. Coil 33°, in **Coil's Masonic Encyclopedia** (p. 520) says: "The prevailing Masonic opinion is that the bible is only a symbol of the divine will, law, or revelation, and not that its contents are divine law, inspired, or revealed. So far, no responsible authority has held that a Freemason must believe the bible or any part of it.

As Freemasonry spread into and among Moslems, Hindus, Brahmans, Buddhists, and other non-Judaic and non-Christian races, none would accept any part of the bible. This made it impossible for the bible to be THE GREAT LIGHT OF MASONRY, as many were urging and reiterating, and led to the device of the VOLUME OF SACRED LAW (V.S.L.), that is, the substitution of a Koran, Veda, the Proverbs of Confucius, or other revered book."

Mrs. E. M. Storms, in her book entitled, **Should a Christian be a Mason**, says, concerning the above statement by Coil: "In other words the bible is not treated in masonry as the Book of God, but rather as a part of the lodge furniture, a symbol on an equal footing with the other sacred books of the various religions of the world.

As a Christian, do you place the bible on an equal footing with the Koran or the Vedas or the Book of Morman? As a Christian, do you think that the will of God is found in those books as it is in the bible? Masonry teaches this, and by doing so deceptively drags the bible down to the level of the other religious books of the world."

Carl Claudy, in **Introduction to Freemasonry**, (p. 38) states: "For the bible is here a symbol of all holy books of all faiths. It is the Masonic way of setting forth the simplest and most profound of truths which Masonry has made so peculiarly her own: that there is a way, there does run a road on which men "of all creeds and of every race" may travel happily together, be their differences of religious faith what they may. In his private devotions a man may petition God or Jehovah, Allah or Buddha, Mohammed or Jesus; he may call upon the God of Israel or the Great First Cause. In the Masonic Lodge he hears humble petition to the Great Architect of the Universe, finding his own deity under that name. A hundred paths may wind upward around a mountain; at the top they meet. Freemasonry opens the Great Light upon her altar not as one book of one faith, but as all books of all faiths."

Notice how the last sentence of Mr. Claudy's statement contradicts the apostle Paul's teaching to the Christians at Ephesus. Eph. 4:5 - "ONE Lord, ONE faith...." Not a dozen different faiths - just ONE!

Rollin C. Blackmer, P.M., P.H.P., in **The Lodge and The Craft** (p. 22) says: "Even with us the Volume of the Sacred Law is regarded more as a symbol of Divine Light than as a rule and guide for faith and practice, and while its presence on the altar as a symbol is considered as indispensable, it is almost never read in the lodge. In thirty years of almost constant attendance at lodge in many jurisdictions, the writer has never heard the Bible read in the lodge, though portions of Scripture are occasionally quoted in the ritualistic work."

Rev. Joseph F. Newton, in **The Men's House**, (pp. 83-84) says: "Thus by the very honor which Masonry pays to the Bible, it teaches us to revere every book of faith in which men find help for today and hope for the morrow, joining hands with the man of Islam as he takes oath on the Koran, and with the Hindu as he makes covenant with God upon the book that he loves best.

For Masons know, what so many forget, that religions are many, but Religion is one. Therefore, it invites to its altar men of all faiths, knowing that, if they use different names for "the Nameless One of a hundred names," they are yet praying to the one God and Father of all; knowing, also, that while they read different volumes, they are in fact reading the same vast Book of Faith of Man as revealed in the struggle and sorrow of the race in its quest of God."

2 John 10-11 *"If there come any unto you, and bring not THIS doctrine, receive him not into your house, neither bid him God speed: For he that biddeth him God speed is partaker of his evil deeds."*

Notice the first sentence of the above statement by Rev. Newton, "Thus by the very HONOR which Masonry pays to the Bible,...." May I ask, what honor? They mutilate the Bible, ignore the Son, take their bloody oaths and obligations upon it, ridicule it's miracles, cast doubt upon it, and drag it down to the same level as other holy books, and all this by a supposedly minister of the gospel. Hell isn't going to be hot enough for men like this.

SECOND - Masonry's doctrinal teachings are all based on the Kabalah, a system of secret theosophy developed by the rabbis from about the seventh to the eighteenth centuries, reaching its peak about the twelfth or thirteenth centuries, and based on a mystical method of interpreting the scriptures to penetrate sacred mysteries and foretell the future.

Albert Pike 33°, in **Morals and Dogma**, (p. 741) says: "Masonry is a search after light. That search leads us directly back, as you see, to the Kabalah (Jewish book of occult knowledge). In that ancient and little understood medley of absurdity and philosophy, the initiate will find the source of many doctrines."

Then on page (744) of the same book, Mr. Pike says: "All truly dogmatic religions have issued from the Kabalah and return to it. Everything scientific and grand in the religious dreams of all the illuminati, Jacob Boehme, Swedenborg, Saint Martin, and others, is borrowed from the Kabalah, all the Masonic associations owe to it their Secrets and their Symbols."

Albert Pike 33°, in **Morals and Dogma**, (pp. 744-745) and J. D. Buck, in **Mystic Masonry**, (p. 42) says: "The Bible, with all the allegories it contains, expresses, in an incomplete and veiled manner only, the religious science of the Hebrews. The doctrine of Moses and the prophets, identical at bottom with that of the ancient Egyptians, also had its outward meaning and its veils. The Hebrew books were written only to recall to memory the traditions; and they were written in symbols unintelligible to the profane. The Pentateuch and the prophets poems were merely elementary books of doctrine, morals or liturgy; and the true secret and traditional philosophy was only written afterward, under a veil still less transparent. Thus was a second Bible born, unknown to, or rather uncomprehended by, the Christians (of later times), a collection, they say, of monstrous absurdities; a monument, the adept says, wherein is every thing that the genius of philosophy and that of religion have ever formed or imagined of the sublime; a treasure surrounded by thorns; a diamond concealed in a rough dark stone. One is filled with admiration on penetrating into the Sanctuary of the Kabalah, at seeing a doctrine so logical, so simple and at the same time so absolute."

Albert Pike 33° in **Morals and Dogma**, (p. 105) says: "The teachers, even of Christianity, are, in general, the most ignorant of the true meaning of that which they teach. There is no book of which so little is known as the Bible. To most who read it, it is as incomprehensible as the Sohar.

And verily must this be the case, since the teachers of Christianity in general are not aware that the Bible is only the Kabalah in another form."

The reason the Bible is so "incomprehensible" to Masons is because they have never really been born-again and do not know Jesus Christ as their personal Saviour.

1 Cor. 2:14 - *"But the natural man receiveth not the things of the spirit of God: for they are foolishness unto him: neither can he know them, because they are spiritually discerned."*

On the other hand, according to J. D. Buck and Albert Pike,- "One is filled with admiration on penetrating into the Sanctuary of the Kabalah, at seeing a doctrine so logical, so simple and at the same time so absolute.

Do you see what the Lodge is trying to imply or teach? There is no book of which so little is known as the Bible - But! the Kabalah is so logical, and so simple, that an idiot (though he be a Mason) can understand it.

Now that makes sense to me, because God the Father is the author of the Bible, and Satan their father, is the author of the Kabalah - they should understand it. In closing I would like to mention that the very foundation of Masonry is the Blue Lodge, and it has nothing to do with the Bible.

G. Wingate Chase, Masonic author, in **Digest of Masonic Law**, (p. 207) says: "Freemasonry calls no man to account for his belief of any religion on the globe. The Jews, the Chinese, the Turks, each reject either the New Testament or the Old Testament, or both, and yet we see no good reason why they should not be made Masons.

In fact Blue Lodge Masonry has nothing whatever to do with the Bible. It is not founded on the Bible; if it were it would not be Masonry; it would be something else.

SALVATION

There is no system but that of the bible, by which man can be saved. This no sober Christian will deny. Masonry is not the system of the bible; therefore it cannot save men, and its pretensions to save them are false. Let a man practice every duty and believe every article of the Masonic creed, and yet he will make his bed in hell, and dwell with devouring flames.

Masonry has no Saviour - no atonement for sin - no repentance toward God - no Holy Spirit - no justification by Christ, and no doctrine of the Trinity, as we know and believe it. Can men be saved by such a system?

Masonry is so shaped and modeled that it exactly pleases the carnal mind, and is designed to bring all classes of men together in a system with which none shall find fault. There is nothing in the whole structure of masonry with which the carnal mind is naturally at enmity, all is gratifying, and equally as gratifying to deists as to any other class of men. To tell men that such a system of religion will save them, is one of the suggestions of the prince of darkness to accomplish their ruin.

If masonry is a system of salvation, and all its pretensions true, how can they be justified in concealing it from any of the human family, especially from women and children. Why should they be left to perish? Why not teach them the whole duty of man, open before them the riches of divine grace in boundless prospect, show them their election of God and their glorified station in his kingdom? It is just as important that they should know and see these things as for anyone else.

The doctrines and precepts of the bible, have no connection whatever with masonry. They belong to the bible and to no other system; they are designed to sanctify and build up the church of God and not a Masonic lodge. What authority, then, have masons for telling the world that masonry teaches the whole duty of man, the same faith and practice with Christianity, and the whole subject matter of divine economy?

From the bible, sinful, fallen man, must take his faith and practice; to this, as to a light which shines in a dark place, the Lord directs him to go and learn his whole duty.

It is not true that Jesus Christ is the spirit and essence, and foundation of the Masonic institution. He has no more to do with it than he has with Mahometanism or paganism. He is the spirit and essence of Christianity and not of masonry; the foundation of the temple of Jehovah and not of the temple of free-masons. We may venture to say, that it is yet a secret to the angels in heaven, that the first promise of a Saviour to this lost world, is the great corner stone in the building of freemasonry.

What! The Saviour of men - the Prince of life - the second person in the adorable Trinity; is he the foundation spirit, and essence of that system of religion, which is nothing more than an amalgamation of pagan superstitions and Jewish ceremonies? How many of the fraternity are avowed deists, openly ridicule the doctrine of the Trinity, the Deity, and vicarious sufferings of Christ? Let Christ crucified be preached in Masonic lodges: and masons urged by the terror of the Lord, by the fire which is prepared for the devil and his angels, to believe in him; what a scattering; what a falling away there would be!

I may be told that the things which I dispute are supported by Masonic tradition. What are Masonic traditions? Who will be so gullible as to embrace a pretended system of religion, which is supported by nothing but Masonic traditions? I have read a remarkable story about the preservation of the five books of Moses, by masons, when the Israelites were carried captive into Babylon. We have another of a similar nature, concerning Enoch.

Thomas Smith Webb, in **Webb's Monitor**, (pp. 270-271) says: "Enoch, being inspired by the Most High, and in commemoration of a wonderful vision, built a temple under ground, and dedicated the same to God. Methuselah, the son of Enoch, constructed the building, without being acquainted with his father's motives. This happened in that part of the world which was afterwards called the land of Canaan, and since known by the name of the Holy Land."

What wonderful sayings can a man support by traditions. Have masons never read what has been written by the infallible dictates of the Holy Spirit? "Thus have ye made the commandment of God, of none effect by your tradition;" "For laying aside the commandment of God, ye hold the tradition of men;" "Full well ye reject the commandment of God that ye may keep your own tradition." In view of these scriptures, Masonic traditions deserve but little credit. What is the saving power of masonry then? It is just what it would be, without the precepts and doctrines which have been detached from the bible. It is as unable to save, as if there were no bible in existence.

Edmond Ronayne, Past Master of Keystone Lodge in Chicago says in **The Master's Carpet**, (p. 63-64) "Taking the very best possible view of freemasonry, is there any one single doctrine, or any one duty inculcated and enforced by the Masonic philosophy, which is not found to be inculcated by God's law and within the pale of the Christian church? *"The church of the living God is the pillar and the ground of the truth,"* (1 Tim. 3:15) which the Lord Jesus Christ has *"sanctified and cleansed with the washing of water by the word, that he might present it to himself a glorious church not having spot or wrinkle or any such thing, but that it* *should be holy and without blemish,"* (Eph. 5:26-27) Can this be said of the Masonic institution? Is that miserable system of sin and folly "without spot or wrinkle?" And are the laws and precepts of Freemasonry, its obligations, death penalties, and its foul philosophy of selfishness, deceit, and cunning, "holy and without blemish?" Why, to compare the church of God to Masonry would be about the same as comparing the brightness of the sun to the darkness of midnight, or the glory of the Mount of Transfiguration to the blackness of despair in the regions of eternal woe. Upon what hypothesis then can a professing Christian, and more especially a Christian minister, justify his conduct in connecting himself with the Masonic institution, and in swearing to support its laws, rules and edicts, whether "right or wrong?"

J. S. M. Ward 33°, in **Freemasonry: Its Aims and Ideals**, (p. 187) says: "The aim of Freemasonry is to combat atheism and gross materialism, to set men's feet on the path of salvation. Freemasonry has taught that each man can by himself, work out his own conception of God, and thereby achieve salvation."

H. L. Haywood, Masonic author, in **The Great Teachings of Masonry**, (pp. 30-31) says: "Masonic initiation is a blessing, carrying with it many precious privileges, and it is therefore worth something of an effort on the part of a man who seeks it.

For consider what takes place inside a man when initiation has been a success. The word itself suggest a "new birth." The experience, whenever it actually occurs, is a profound one.

It is like the moral and spiritual change which comes over a man who passes through the religious experience known as "conversion or regeneration;"

Masonic initiation is intended to be quite as profound and as revolutionizing an experience. As a result of it the candidate should become a new man.

The whole purpose of the ritual, of the symbols, of all that is done and said, is solemnly to bring about such a transformation in the man. If initiation does not accomplish something of this it is a failure; if it does accomplish it, that fact should forever silence those who have looked upon it as an elaborate and expensive piece of formalism."

W. L. Wilmshurst, P.M., in **The Meaning of Masonry**, (p. 35) says: "The ceremony of our first degree, then, is a swift and comprehensive portrayal of the entrance of all men into, first, physical life, and second, into spiritual life; and as we extend congratulations when a child is born into the world, so also we receive with acclamation the candidate for Masonry who, symbolically, is seeking for spiritual re-birth; and herein we emulate what is written of the joy that exists among the angels of heaven over every sinner who repents and turns towards the light. The first degree is also eminently the degree of preparation, of self-discipline and purification. It corresponds with that symbolical cleansing accorded in the sacrament of Baptism."

On (p. 42) of the same book, Mr. Wilmshurst says: "All that has happened in the third degree is that he (the candidate) has symbolically passed through a great and striking change: a rebirth, or regeneration of his whole nature. He has been "sown a corruptible body;" and in virtue of the self-discipline and self-development he has undergone, there has been raised in him "an incorruptible body, " and death has been swallowed up in the victory he has attained over himself."

Again, on (p. 46) of the same book, Mr. Wilmshurst says: "To sum up the import of the teaching of the three degrees, it is clear, therefore, that from grade to grade the candidate is being led from an old to an entirely new quality of life. He begins his Masonic career as the natural man; he ends it by becoming through its DISCIPLINE a regenerated perfected man. To attain this transmutation, this metamorphosis of himself, he is taught first to purify and subdue his sensual nature; then to purify and develop his mental nature; and finally, by utter surrender of his old life and losing his soul to save it, he rises from the dead a Master, a just man made perfect, with larger consciousness and faculties, an efficient instrument for use by the Great Architect in His plan of rebuilding the Temple of fallen humanity, and capable of initiating and advancing other men to a participation in the same great work."

J. D. Buck, in **Mystic Masonry**, (p. 86) says: "All real initiation is an internal, not an external process. The outer ceremony is dead and useless only so far as it symbolizes and illustrates, and thereby makes clear the inward change. The ceremony instructs, but it can not transform. To transform means to regenerate; and this comes by trial, by effort, by self-conquest, by sorrow, disappointment, failure; and a daily renewal of the conflict. It is thus that man must work out his own salvation."

Isn't it sad and terrible when ungodly men lead other men into the very pits of hell with their damnable doctrine; teaching them salvation by works rather than trusting in the Lord Jesus Christ and his finished work on Calvary? But this isn't hard to understand though in the light of the following scripture.

2 Peter 2:1-3 *"But there were false prophets also among the people, even as there shall be false teachers among you, who secretly shall bring in destructive heresies, even denying the Lord that bought them, and bring upon themselves swift destruction. And many shall follow their pernicious ways, by reason of whom the way of truth shall be evil spoken of. And through covetousness shall they, with feigned words, make merchandise of you; whose judgment now for a long time lingereth not, and their destruction slumbereth not."*

H. L. Haywood, in **The Great Teachings of Masonry**, (p. 137) says: "At the end of initiation he stands on his own feet, he sees the light, he has in him a new vision, a new nature. Under the veil of symbolism the novice is presented as a shapeless stone, or Rough Ashlar, fresh from the quarry. When the "work" is done he is a Perfect Ashlar, a stone hewn and finished, ready for its place in the wall. If this can happen to a man inside the lodge room it can happen outside; if a man can be BORN AGAIN UNDER MASONIC INFLUENCE, he can also be born again under other equally powerful influences."

Once more, masonry puts the plan of salvation aside,

and in its place puts mere moral teachings enforced by material symbols. This whole system is a plan to DO AWAY WITH THE ATONEMENT OF JESUS CHRIST and to lead the poor sinner to trust man in the awful day of judgment, with no hope except what his miserable, paltry righteousness has been able to get for himself.

Masonry pretends to form the most lovely, the most illustrious moral characters, to fit men for heaven and for its eternal enjoyments; yet it never formed one such character, nor fitted one soul for heaven, nor reclaimed one sinner from the paths of perdition.

There is no person in heaven nor on earth, who can say that he has been turned from sin to holiness, transformed into the image of Christ, made a new creature, made meet to be a partaker of the inheritance of the saints in light, by the influence of masonry. Without this change, no person sustains the Christian character, nor that character which is lovely in the sight of God. This change is wrought and this character formed by the Christian religion, and not by masonry. The Christian religion has formed millions of such characters; but masonry never formed one. Hence, falling short of its highest pretensions, as a religious system, it is one of the greatest delusions ever imposed on the world. Let us continue with masonry's pretensions to save men.

Albert Mackey 33°, in **Lexicon of Freemasonry** (p.16) under the word ACACIAN says: "Acacian - a term signifying a Mason who by living in strict obedience to the obligations and precepts of the fraternity is free from sin."

Can you believe this? A mason can lie under oath, deny Christ as the only Saviour of the world, mutilate the bible, be unequally yoked with unbelievers, and yet be free from sin, by living in strict obedience to the obligations and precepts of the fraternity.

Albert Mackey, in **Masonic Ritualist**, (p. 238) says: "Freemasons mutually promote the welfare and happiness of each other to the honor and glory of God and THE SALVATION OF OUR OWN SOULS."

Daniel Sickels 33°, in **Ahiman Rezon**, (p. 196) says: "We now find man complete in morality and intelligence, with the stay of religion added to insure him of the protection of the deity, and guard him against ever going astray. These three degrees thus form a perfect and harmonious whole; nor can we conceive that anything can be suggested more, which the soul of man requires."

Masonry teaches salvation - but they do not teach salvation by faith, nor by the vicarious atonement. Let us continue. J. D. Buck, in Mystic Masonry, (p.57) says: "Every soul must 'work out its own salvation', and 'take the kingdom of heaven by force'. Salvation by faith and the vicarious atonement were not taught, as now interpreted by Jesus, nor are these doctrines taught in the esoteric scriptures. They are later and ignorant perversions of the original doctrines ."

Before closing on the subject of "Salvation", I would like to mention that Masonry claims to be one of the HOLIEST INSTITUTIONS known to mankind.

Albert Mackey 33°, in **Manual of the Lodge**, (p. 61) says: "NO institution was ever raised on a better principle or more solid foundation; nor were ever more excellent rules and useful maxims laid down than are inculcated in the several Masonic lectures."

Rev. Joseph F. Newton, in **The Men's House**, (p. 151) says: "The story of Masonry is one of the great romances of the world. Older then our Republic, older than any living religion, it has come to us out of the mists of the past, one of the HOLIEST INSTITUTIONS known to mankind".

I do not see how the good reverend could make such a statement about this ungodly, satanic institution, in the light of what the bible has to say on HOLINESS.

Did the Lord ever pour out his Spirit upon Masonic lodges and produce revivals in them, like those we have witnessed in the Church of God?

Is it not remarkable that we should be told that masonry "embraces the whole subject matter of divine economy"; that it "embraces and inculcates evangelical truth"; yet the

Lord never owned and blessed it by the outpouring of his Spirit upon its members?

It is pretended, as we have already seen, that the ancient druids, the priests and philosophers of all heathen nations, understood and taught the mysteries of masonry. This being the case, and masonry "embracing the whole subject matter of divine economy, and inculcating evangelical truth;" why did not those priests and philosophers evangelize the world and reclaim it from idolatry? Why were they idolators themselves? Plainly, because masonry is not what it professes to be. Will not evangelical truth and the whole subject matter of divine economy, reform men and reclaim them from idolatry? They will; they have done it, and are continuing to do it: but masonry has never done it, and never can do it.

SPIRITUAL LIGHT

The Church, the minister, the Christian is a watchman on the walls, and it is his business to see the threatening enemy when his spear-point comes over the top of the hill, that the gates may be shut, the walls manned, the men armed, and women and children protected. It is the business of the watchman to look out not for pleasant but FOR INJURIOUS THINGS, and to point them out.

If you go into a dark room filled with creeping things, you cannot see anything, but if you light a match, you see some of those creatures; if you light a lamp, you see more; and, if you turn on an electric light, it reveals all the little creatures. "That which doth make manifest is light," and the Christian is the light of the world. The Church establishes the moral standard for men who never go near it, and for communities who reject it!

George L. Hunt, in **Secret Societies**, (p. 16) says: "The Holy Spirit on the day of Pentecost openly proclaimed through the disciples an accomplished atonement by Jesus Christ and opened wide the doors of the church to all that would come in. But Masonry, if it has any light, selfishly puts it under a bushel and sells it out to a select few candidates at so much a degree. Every Christian who goes knocking at the doors of a Masonic lodge seeking for light, thereby denies that Jesus Christ is the light, and by this act testifies that Jesus is not enough to illuminate his soul, and in order to receive the light of masonry is willing to enter into any kind of an oath, or submit to any indignity, that may be demanded of him. All this puts Christ to an open shame and leads the unconverted to believe that the light of Christianity is insufficient."

Albert Mackey 33°, in **Manual of the Lodge**, (p. 20) says: "There he (the candidate) stands, without our portals, on the threshold of his new Masonic life, in darkness, helplessness and ignorance. Having been wandering amid the errors, and covered over with the pollutions of the outer and profane world, he comes inquiringly to our doors, seeking the new birth, and asking a withdrawal of the veil..."

George Stienmetz, in **Freemasonry - Its Hidden Meaning**, (p. 102) says: "Not satisfied with the light, or knowledge, he has so far obtained, of his own free will and accord, he gives the knock which will cause the door to be opened for him to begin his journey for FURTHER LIGHT in Freemasonry."

We see the candidate here seeking "further light". Masonry is a never-ending search for LIGHT, always promised but never quite realized. 2 Tim. 3:7 - *"Ever learning and never able to come to the knowledge of the truth."*

In Scottish Rite Masonry, Vol. 1 (p. 146); in the Eighth Degree, Intendant of the Building, we find the candidate still in darkness and acknowledging his ignorance.

Solomon - How were you received?

Tito - By acknowledging my ignorance.

Solomon - Why were you raised to that degree?

Tito - In order to dispel the darkness in which I was immersed, and to get such light as would regulate my heart and enlighten my understanding.

It seems to me, according to this, that the further you go in Masonry, the greater is the darkness and ignorance. Matt. 6:23 - *"If therefore the light that is in thee be darkness, how great is that darkness"!*

Albert Mackey 33°, in **Manual of the Lodge**, (p. 93) and Daniel Sickels 33°, in **Ahiman Rezon**, (p. 169) says: "It is one of the most beautiful, but at the same time one of the most abstruse doctrines of the science of Masonic symbolism that the Mason is ever to be in search of truth, but is never to find it".

This reminds me of the story about the donkey who was always struggling to reach that illusive carrot hanging on a stick out in front of him, as he plowed the field.

Finally we come to the Thirty-second degree, the final earned degree of the Scottish Rite. In Scottish Rite Masonry, under Lecture of the 32nd Degree, we read: "You have reached the mountain peak of Masonic instruction, a peak covered with mist, which YOU in search for further light can penetrate only by your own efforts."

Thus we see, that a Masonic candidate seeking light, must knock on a separate door for each desired degree. Finally after going through thirty-two doors and reaching the peak of Masonic instruction, a peak covered with mist, we find the candidate, as much in the dark now, as he ever was before.

Mr. Runquist, in **The Cross or the Compass** (p. 6), says: "A man who has taken all Thirty-three degrees of Masonry and been in the lodge most of his life, doesn't have as much light as a ten year old boy who can quote John 3:16. John 8:12 - *"Then spake Jesus again unto them, saying, I am the light of the world: he that FOLLOWETH ME shall not walk in darkness, but shall have the light of life."*

THE FATHERHOOD OF GOD AND THE BROTHERHOOD OF MAN

Alphonse Cerza, Masonic author, in his book entitled, **Let There Be Light** (p. 45), says: "The moral teachings of Freemasonry are in no way opposed to the gentle beliefs of Christianity. It is not possible to find any lesson taught in the ceremonies of Freemasonry that can be called anti-Christian. The basic principles of Freemasonry are the Fatherhood of God and the Brotherhood of Man. Are these not also the basic principles of Christianity?

If Alphonse Cerza had been a Christian, and had accepted Jesus Christ as his personal Saviour, and had been truly born-again, he would know the answer to that question.

By nature men are creatures of God, but not children of God. We all descended from the same source, the same parents, the same Mother Eve. In Acts 17:26 the apostle Paul is preaching at Athens, and he says to the people that God *"hath made of one blood all nations of men for to dwell on all the face of the earth."* Does that mean that all men are the children of God?

You say, "I know that I'm a child of God because God created me." Then a cow is a child of God in exactly the same sense that you are, for God created the cow, too.

The bible clearly teaches that all men by nature are sinners. Eph. 2:3 - *"...and were by nature the children of wrath, even as others."* The misconception comes in when the lodge teaches, that because God created us, we are his children. This isn't true; if you are unconverted, you are not akin to God, but akin to your father, the Devil. We are plainly told in Rom. 9:8 - *"They which are the children of the flesh, these ARE NOT the children of God..."*

Now that question came up with Jesus. Jesus talked one time to some people who claimed to be God's children. They had this idea of the universal Fatherhood of God. Jesus talked to the Pharisees. John 8:41 - *"Ye do the deeds of your father. Then said they to him, We be not born of fornication; we have one Father, even God."* See, they are claiming to be children of one father - God. "We have one Father," they said, John 8:42,43 - *"Jesus said unto them, If God were your Father, ye would love me: for I proceeded forth and came from God; neither came I of myself, but he sent me. Why do ye not understand my speech? even because ye cannot hear my word."* He that is of God heareth God's word. Jesus continuing said, *"Ye are of your father the devil, and the lust of your father ye will do. He was a murderer from the beginning, and abode not in the truth, because there is no truth in him. When he speaketh a lie, he speaketh of his own: for he is a liar, and the father of it."* Jesus said - "Why do ye not understand my speech?" Masons cannot understand Jesus any more than the pharisees could, and Paul tells us why in 1 Cor. 2:14 - *"But the natural man receiveth not the things of the spirit of God: for they are foolishness unto him: neither can he know them, because they are spiritually discerned."*

Joseph F. Newton, in **The Men's House** (pp. 41-42), says: "For if there be a God at all, who is the life of all that was, is, and is to be, that God must be the Father of all mankind; and if we are all born into this world by one high wisdom and one vast love, then we are brothers to the last man of us, forever. For better for worse, for richer for poorer in sickness and in health, till death do us part, men are held together by ties of spiritual kinship, sons of one eternal Father."

I would like to ask Mr. Newton where do these ties of spiritual kinship come from, and what makes us sons of one eternal Father? The answer is given in the following two scriptures: John 1:11-13 *"As many as RECEIVED HIM to them gave He power to become the SONS OF GOD....who were BORN OF GOD."* and Gal. 3:26 - *"Ye are all children of God BY FAITH IN CHRIST JESUS."*

It is sad that so many who THINK themselves children of God, are in reality children of the Devil. Jesus said in Matt. 7:21 - *"Not every one that saith unto me, Lord, Lord, shall enter into the kingdom of heaven; but he that doeth the will of my Father which is in heaven."* Now what is the will of the Father? Jesus has answered that for us in John 6:40- *"And this is the will of him that sent me, that every one which seeth the Son and believeth on him, may have everlasting life: and I will raise him up at the last day."*

The only real "brotherhood of man" that the bible speaks about is that which comes about by trusting in the shed blood of Christ on Calvary.

H. L. Haywood, in **The Great Teachings of Masonry** (p. 120), says: "All men, whatever be their faith or fortune, from Plato down to the African dwarf, HAVE THIS RELATION WITH GOD. What God is to any one, He is to every other one; and all that God can be to or do for any man, He is to and does for all men equally and everlastingly. This eternal and universal Fatherhood in Him does not come into existence when we begin to believe it; it is already a fact before we believe it, and remains a fact whether we believe it or not."

This is another lie of the devil, right out of the pits of hell! No wonder Jesus said in Matt. 23:15 - *"Woe unto you, scribes and Pharisees, hypocrites* (and Masons!) *for ye compass sea and land to make one proselyte and when he is made, ye make him twofold more the child of hell than yourselves."*

Masonry teaches a brotherhood of the unregenerate, they teach the ability of the unregenerate to approach God in prayer. If a Buddhist, Hindu, or Moslem rejects Jesus Christ as his personal Saviour, then, as far as the bible is concerned, he is lost. If he is lost, then he is a sinner, and John 9:31 says - *"Now we know that God heareth not sinners"*. All the prayers that this individual prays, will be in vain UNLESS it is a prayer of repentance.

In closing I would like to give an example of Masonic brotherhood in relation to Christian brotherhood. In all of the monitors, guides and rituals I have, they give a set distance that a mason is to travel in rendering service to a brother, and it varies from about three miles for an Entered Apprentice to about forty miles for the degrees of Knighthood.

I'm glad that in the church of God we are not bound by any length of cable-tow, as to how far we are to go in helping a brother or sister in need. The length that we can go in helping others is determined by the love of God and it knows no bounds - they don't make a cable-tow that long.

The fellowship of saints is far more close and binding than that of the lodge. There is no real brotherhood outside of the church and apart from Jesus Christ. The fellowship of the lodge, based on oaths, obligations, and threats of repulsive mutilations and hideous deaths, has no true love in it, and cannot compare with the fellowship and brotherly love which is experienced by those who are born again and have been adopted into the family of God. Can you imagine Jesus threatening his disciples with those terrible penalties (plucking out their hearts, tearing their tongues out by the roots, and cutting their throats from ear to ear) for repeating some of the things he told them not to tell? If you want to see a good example of brotherly love, read the parable of the Good Samaritan in Luke 10:30-37.

Chapter 10

AN ADDRESS TO THE FOLLOWERS OF CHRIST BELONGING TO THE MASONIC LODGE

What possible motives can induce Christians to become masons? Are they influenced by a desire to promote the glory of God and the good of their fellow men? Will the glory of God influence his children to swear solemn allegiance to a worldly institution. Do you believe, my brethren, that the Lord ever smiled on an individual saint when he saw him joining the lodge, and taking the awful oaths of a mason? Do you believe that a man who takes these obligations upon him, can fulfill them, and also fulfill those of a Christian? Do you believe that a Christian and especially a minister, is justified in solemnly swearing in such a manner, as to place himself in circumstances where he cannot, on all occasions, appear as a witness against a mason, nor act against him, either before the church or the civil authorities without violating his obligations?

The love of human applause, of popular distinction, of being made acquainted with something new and mysterious, are motives which often exert a powerful influence on our depraved hearts. These things allure and fascinate the multitude. Christians who fall in love with masonry, have reason to question whether they have not been led astray by these enchanting delusions. A mason is thought by a certain class to be honorable, and to be marked with a kind of mysterious and unknown distinction. These are temptations the human heart is always seeking, and with which it is always ready to comply.

Do Christians become masons that they may be more wise in a knowledge of divine things? Does not the bible contain all the wisdom and moral instruction any one can need? Has not God revealed to us, in the holy book, all he intends we shall know of moral subjects in this state of things? Does masonry teach any thing true about God, and about Jesus Christ and the mystery of redemption, which the bible does not? Is God so partial to masons as to reveal some deep mystery to them, which he has never revealed to the church? Why then, should men go to masonry for moral instruction? Are they any wiser? Are their hearts any better? Are there not those who are as much distinguished for their knowledge in divine things as masons, yet have never been taught within the walls of a Masonic lodge? The bible contains all that ministers need to know and teach, and all that Christians need to know and practice, and is able to make men wise unto salvation. 2 Peter 1:3 *"According as his divine power hath given unto us **all** things that pertain unto life and godliness, through the knowledge of him that hath called us to glory and virtue."*

Are Christians more useful for becoming masons? Some may think they are. Masonry adds nothing to their influence in the cause of God, nor to their worth in the church. Rev. Forrest DeLoss Haggard 33°, in his book entitled **The Clergy and the Craft** (p. 9) states - "We are sure that he who is true to the principles he learns in Freemasonry will be a better church member because of it. I have heard more than one minister say that he felt he was a better Christian and a better minister because of his Freemasonry."

I cannot believe this. Ministers preach no better. Their sermons are not more powerful, affectionate, and edifying, and have no more of Christ and the Holy Spirit in them. They do not appear to possess any more eagerness for souls, and the glory of the Saviour, nor any more of the Holy Spirit, nor to be more prayerful and godly, nor to live nearer the cross of Christ, for being masons. What advantage then, is it, for men to be masons and to betray Christ? Could the prestige of the 33rd degree, be as tempting to the Rev. Forrest DeLoss Haggard, as the thirty pieces of silver was to Judas? In what sense are they better Christians or ministers? Where is the balance of good which they could not accomplish, did they sustain no other character than disciples of Christ, and no other name than Christians?

Some ministers may tell interesting stories, about being received and treated with the utmost kindness and respect among strangers, because they were masons. Will this justify them in becoming masons; and is it an evidence that it renders them more useful? Could they tell us of souls they have converted to God among masons?

When ministers meet with masons in Masonic lodges, they often meet with the assemblies of the ungodly; and with men who are rude and vain and worldly minded, and whose filthy conversation on many occasions would vex the soul of a righteous Lot. With these men they associate in the most familiar manner - they call them brethren and acknowledge them as such, as much as they do the followers of Christ. What satisfaction can they take in such a society? Have they a relish for it? Are they at home among such men? Are they one people and have they one God and saviour? And are they called in one hope of their calling? Is this the influence which masonry has on the minds of Christians, to attach them to wicked men and make them fond of their society? 2 Cor. 6:17 *"Wherefore come out from among them, and be ye separate, saith the Lord, and touch not the unclean thing; and I will receive you."* Also 2 Tim. 2:19 *"Let everyone that nameth the name of Christ depart from iniquity."*

Do ministers pretend that on some occasions they have larger assemblies to hear the word, then they would were they not masons? Even if this were true - is this sufficient proof that these measures are lawful, and that God justifies ministers in becoming masons?

There are many ministers of Christ, who are as active and as useful at home and abroad, and meet with as great success in the ministry, and will accomplish as much good before they go home to rest, from their labors, as those who are masons, yet have never seen the "riches of divine grace opened before them in boundless prospect" in a Masonic lodge.

What are the ministers of Christ preaching to the world? The great burden of their ministry is to show men the absolute necessity of renouncing all dependence on an arm of flesh, and of trusting wholly in the faithfulness of a covenant keeping God. Do they reduce this to practice? Do they exhibit to the world an unshaken confidence in the arm of Jehovah? If not, of what use is their preaching? Can they expect that others will be influenced by it? When they resort to a worldly institution for protection or support, they trust in man and make flesh their arm; they virtually cast away the precious promises of the bible, and distrust the truth of the omnipotent Saviour, who has pledged himself to be with them "always even unto the end of the world." If ministers are not willing to trust God among strangers, in a strange land, and to trust their ministry in his hands unless they become masons, they need to pray for more faith; and perhaps would be better in some other calling, in which they would venture to take God at his word.

That men of the world should be inspired with love of masonry is not surprising; for it is every way adapted to their self-righteous and aspiring views. But that holy men of God should be caught in its snares, is truly inexplainable. From the false charms which are thrown around the institution, some ministers may believe that joining it will enlarge the sphere of their usefulness. But I personally believe that the greater part are actuated by motives which the gospel of Christ does not sanction. To pretend that joining this institution, facilitates the cultivation and enlargement of the human mind, is absurd. For those who can tell us the whole story about masonry, with the familiarity a school boy would his lesson, stand no higher on the hill of science than hundreds and thousands of others who have no knowledge of masonry, and are men of inferior attainments. And to say that God has communicated divine truths to Masonic lodges, which he has withheld from the church of Christ, is blasphemous. One grand motive governs most of those who become masons. They are fascinated with the idea of being popular among the great and wise ones of the world; and of having these men pledged on oath to support their interest in the greatest distress. To secure this popularity and the friendship and support of this class of men, is the highest motive which influences most, if not all ministers who become masons.

This is treating the promises of God with contempt. The language which the Masonic lodge holds out to ministers is, "join us and we will help support you." Will the promises of Almighty God fail those who carry in their hands a commission which bears on it the broad seal of heaven? Will not the solemn and repeated pledges which he has made them, warrant the exercise of an unshaken faith? Why then should they enter into a covenant with the world, to obtain a support in the high calling of the ministry? "O ye of little faith!" Shall ministers be afraid or ashamed to be poor like their divine Master, who, when going about preaching the gospel of the kingdom, had no where to lay his head? "The disciple is not above his master, nor the servant above his lord."

It is treating the cross with contempt. Ministers should anticipate the greatest share of the reproach, contempt and sufferings of the cross. But the league which they form with masons, is designed to wipe off this reproach, to do away with these sufferings and to render the cross a mere popular thing. It is a method which Satan has invented, by which ministers of Christ may pass through the world, shielded from the offence of the cross. "Join us," say masons, "and you will be respected by all classes of men!" Enchanting delusion! How many has it caught? Shall ministers be ashamed to suffer for Christ, and to bear in their bodies the dying of the Lord Jesus? "God forbid," says Paul, "that I should glory, save in the cross of our Lord Jesus Christ."

It is securing the friendship of the world. Good ministers of Christ, who are not masons, enjoy the friendship of the church and of all good beings. What more can they wish? That friendship which they secure by becoming masons, is emphatically "the friendship of the world," and "is enmity with God."

Ministers are overseers of the flock of God. Ought they not to prize its interest above every other object? If they do not, is the flock secure under their care? Is it safe trusting the concerns of the flock in the hands of those who have sworn an allegiance to its enemies? There is danger that on some occasions, the interest of the flock may be sacrificed; and that some of the innocent lambs may be decoyed into the wilderness, among beasts of prey.

The greatest obligations possible, are resting on ministers of God, to labor with untiring diligence to promote the salvation of men; by exhibiting to the world that system, which infinite wisdom has adapted to compel men from the strong holds of sin, and to lead them to an entire dependence on the mediation of the Son of God. Masonic ministers, in many instances do the reverse. They nourish the pride of self-righteous hearts.

Masonry is a self-righteous system, and every effort which they make to support and recommend it to the world as a system of morality, is contributing to the perdition of men. They encourage men in that which the Lord condemns, and over which he has hung his heaviest curses. The pretended moral edifice which they labor to erect, is emphatically a refuge of lies and a strong hold of Satan.

From the nature of Masonic obligations it must be considered that Christians who take these obligations upon them, and pursue masonry, violate their Christian covenant. A mason must consider himself more solemnly pledged to masons than to Christians, and to the lodge than to the church. Masons are the first and highest objects of his regard.

When Christians give themselves to God, and their brethren, they make no reservations; all they have they give to Christ, and to the church. What then have they left to give to masonry? Brethren! When under the influence of the Holy Spirit, with hearts warmly attached to God and his people, you swore allegiance to the King of Zion, could you, at the same time and on the same day, have joined a Masonic lodge, and have taken upon you the awful oaths of a mason?

Those Christians who are more fondly attached to the society of masons than to that of the people of God, and are willing to venture the awful experiment of being involved in the ruins of the Masonic edifice, must be left to pursue their unyielding way. But Almighty God solemnly reminds us all, that "He will bring every work into judgment, with every secret thing," "In the day when God shall judge the secrets of men by Jesus Christ."

Chapter 11

AN ADDRESS TO CHURCHES

The subject of Freemasonry is of utmost importance as far as the church is concerned. Such is its nature, that no society of people, of whatever denomination, who call themselves a Christian church, can, with propriety, remain neutral. For, if masonry be what it professes, if "The principles of speculative free-masonry have the same co-eternal and unshaken foundation, contain and inculcate the same truths in substance, and propose the same ultimate end as the doctrines of Christianity;" if in a Masonic lodge a good man "discovers his election to, and his glorified station in, the kingdom of his Father; " and sees the riches of divine grace opened in boundless prospect, and that all the heavenly sojourners will be admitted within the veil of God's presence; it deserves to be hailed and patronized by all the churches of God; and every Christian ought to join a Masonic lodge, and all who oppose masonry ought to be excluded from the church. But on the other hand, if these pretensions are not true, if masonry is what it obviously appears to be, as quoted by their own authors and teachers, and as outlined in their books on ritual and history, it is an evil; and no church can be justifiable in withholding its aid to stop its progress.

There are some churches which have been informed of the corrupt nature and evil tendency of the Masonic institution! They have seen wicked men encouraged to build their hopes for heaven on their own righteousness; they have seen an alarming union daily forming between the church and the world; they have seen Christians strangely infatuated with the love of masonry, manifesting a greater regard for an institution of the world than for the church of the living god. It is high time to exhort those who are in connection with free-masonry, to come out and be separate.

Some churches remain indifferent; others are disposed to

think favorably, and in some instances to advocate the cause of masonry.

Has it not been shown in preceding chapters, that masonry pretends to be a system of religion, and that it makes the same pretensions as the bible, even to save men and fit them for the society and the enjoyments of heaven? And has it not also been shown, that all those religious pretensions are false?

Will churches of our Lord be indifferent to this? Will they plead for it and call it a good thing? Are they willing that their ministers and leading members should take an active part in propagating this false system and seducing men to believe it? Those who have joined the lodge, are contributing their influence to support a system which is no less false, absurd, and deceptive than the system of Mahomet. If churches remain indifferent, and take no measures to check the progress of this mighty evil, will their garments be found clean at the judgment day?

We have seen that the principles of masonry and of Christianity are perfectly at war. The spirit of masonry is a spirit of selfishness; that of Christianity is a spirit of benevolence; masons view their institution as superior to the institutions of Christ; that of Christ acknowledge no superior: masons are more solemnly pledged to masons than to Christians; Christians are more solemnly pledged to Christians than to masons. Such is the clashing nature of each system, that so far as men submit to the control of one they must cast off that of the other.

Is it agreeable to the holy scriptures, that the wicked and the righteous, the church and the world should be joined together as brethren? Is this pleasing to God? Will he own and bless it, and will he own and bless those churches which advocate it? "My kingdom is not of this world;" "Wherefore come out from among them, and be ye separate, saith the Lord;" "Who is she that looketh forth as the morning, fair as the moon, clear as the sun, and terrible as an army with banners?"

It is often said "that many professedly good men of all

denominations, are masons, and some of them say, that masonry is a good moral institution - that its obligations are perfectly consistent with the obligations of Christianity. Shall we not put confidence in these men? Would they not have renounced and exposed the institution were it corrupt?" This has influenced the minds of a vast many. - While they see professedly good men joining this society, contributing their influence to support it, and often hear them commend it as a virtuous system, they are naturally led to inquire can it be corrupt? The conduct of such men is a mystery to all who have given it a serious investigation. That men who profess a supreme relish for moral excellence, above all, that ministers of Jesus Christ, should be so charmed with heathenish, Jewish, and profane ceremonies - ceremonies, which convey no useful information to any being on earth - and are not even worthy the notice of children - that they should be so infatuated with a system which is supported by the most barbarous and outlandish oaths, is one of the greatest wonders that has ever been exhibited on the theater of this fallen world. Professedly good men are not infallible; and so far as light has gone abroad on the subject, the public are prepared to say, that these men have been deceived and have greatly erred. The attachment of thousands of such men to the Masonic lodge, is no evidence of its being pure, but is a great evidence of human depravity. If these men would renounce and expose masonry were it corrupt, why will they, when the whited wall is broken down, and people are beginning to discover the rottenness and the dead men's bones which have been concealed for ages, I say, why will many of them labor to cover the putrid mass and to prevent the exposure? They are unwilling that masonry should come to light, and that the public should judge for themselves. Must we depend on these men to give us correct views of the institution, when they are manifestly under a very great deception? They tell us that masonry is the same in substance with Christianity; yet those men who are the most zealously attached to the fraternity, and even dare to put at defiance the laws of our country to defend it, have no more reverence for the word and institutions of Jehovah, than they have for the productions of Mahomet.

It is said "that masonry is something we know nothing about; it is therefore best to be silent on the subject, for it produces unpleasantness and even contention among brethren." Has masonry never been "unveiled," it is not true that we know nothing about it. Though most individuals may not know what are the secret signs and ceremonies of the order, yet they can as well judge of its moral nature and tendency, as the nature and tendency of the Christian religion. Masons have written and published volumes on this subject. If, after all this, it must be said that we remain ignorant, it must be admitted that their publications deserve no credit. True, it produces a great deal of unpleasantness among brethren. But is this an evidence that nothing ought to be said on the subject? If so, Christians must lay aside "the whole armor of God," and no longer "contend earnestly for the faith once delivered to the saints." Nothing must be said on any subject which produces unpleasant feelings, however important it may be to the glory of God, and the advancement of Christ's kingdom. A contention for truth will always produce unpleasantness in the minds of those who do not love truth. The preaching of Stephen caused some of his hearers, to" gnash on him with their teeth;" and even to take his life,

Again, it is frequently said, "that we can not discipline church members for being masons, unless they are guilty of immoral conduct". This supposes that church members cannot be disciplined for their sentiments. They may embrace what sentiments they please, turn Mahometans, papists, or Jews, yet they cannot be disciplined, unless they are guilty of immoral conduct. Some reasons will be offered why church members who belong to the Masonic lodge may be considered the subjects of discipline, unless they renounce their connection with it.

Their connection with that institution, tends to weaken confidence in them. They cannot fulfill their Masonic obligations and pursue a course of Christian honesty. On some occasions they must unlawfully conceal facts, or misrepresent them, or flatly deny them, or violate an oath.

They belong to a society which embraces a multitude of profane and immoral characters, who are in every sense men of the world, with whom a free association is incompatible with Christian purity.

The oaths which they take, afford a sufficient reason why they should be disciplined. They swear away their lives and all they have into the hands of masons, and cannot consider themselves the property of the church nor of their country, but of the Masonic institution. Their oaths suppose, that they are at liberty to speak evil of all who are not masons, and to wrong all who are not masons. To do these things to any extent they please, is no violation of their Masonic obligations. The oath by which they are bound to be chaste, carries on the very face of it, the strongest possible indication that they are under no obligation to regard the purity of any females, but those whom they "know" to be the wife, sister, or daughter of a master mason. To violate the chastity of all others, is no violation of this oath. The organization to which they belong and which they support, cannot maintain its discipline without sacrificing the rights of free men, and putting at defiance the laws of the land.

Should the grand lodge of this state, become ever so wicked and lawless, they are bound by oath to support their constitution.

Should the by-laws, rules, and regulations, of any lodge to which they might at any time belong, be decidedly opposed to the laws of the church of God, and require a course of unchristian conduct, they are under oath to conform to them.

Should they be required by a master mason to go on his errand, and should this be to assist him in an unjust cause, they are bound to, if they have to go barefoot and bareheaded.

By swearing to keep the secrets of a master mason, there may be many instances in which they cannot testify against him, though required to by the church or by the laws of the country. Men who take such an oath and do not renounce it, cannot expect a great share of the confidence of others.

The oaths, by which they are bound to assist those of the fraternity, divide their superior obligations to those who are of the household of faith, and place the interest of masonry above every other.

It may be said by masons that they do not view their obligations in this light; that they are misrepresented. The question is not how they view the nature of their oaths; but it is this - what is their nature? To determine this, we are not to be guided by the views of masons, but by the very letter and spirit of their oaths.

Every master mason mimics death. He professes to be killed in imitation of Hiram Abiff. Masons, in a mock way, knock him down, kill him, and lay him aside for a dead man. How does a Christian look in this ceremony, fooling with death and the winding sheet? What an appearance does a minister make, wrapped in a shroud and laid away for a dead man?

They wear mock titles. The title high priest, as worn by them, is mockery. Their priesthood is a perpetuation of the levitical priesthood; and its meaning is, if it has any, Christ has not yet come. Some ministers who preach that Christ has come, and that the whole law dispensation is done away, have put on the robes of Aaron and assumed the title, high priest of God. This practice says that the gospel is a delusion and its author an imposter.

They are guilty of profaneness. They make a profane use of the name of God, of the holy scriptures, of the title, high priest, and of the sanctum sanctorum. In the lecture on the third degree, "a master's lodge is said to represent the sanctum sanctorum, or holy of holies in king Solomon's temple." What a profanation of holy things!

They must be viewed as covenant breakers. For, according to their oaths, they are the property of the Masonic institution, and their earthly substance is devoted to promote the interest of that institution in preference to any other. Their Masonic obligations are, in their nature, superior to all others, and are manifestly designed to secure to those who take them, privileges which they cannot enjoy but at the expense of the rights of others. Finally, to take such oaths - to belong to such a society - to profane holy things - to mimic death - to wear mock titles - to perpetuate Jewish and heathenish ceremonies - to violate the Christian covenant, is a sin and ungodly. "He that hath an ear let him hear what the spirit saith unto the churches."

Chapter 12

MASONRY FELLOWSHIPPED BY CHURCHES

Masonry pollutes the character of the church of God. Churches of all denominations fellowship the institution. Many of their members belong to the lodge, have taken its sacrilegious oaths, practice its heathenish and profane ceremonies and use their greatest effort to build it up and extend its influence far and wide. There is no class of men who are doing more to support the institution of masonry than members of churches. They are its champions - the pillars on which it rests. They have devoted a considerable amount of time in travelling the country as lecturers in the lodges and chapters. What they do for the lodge has a greater tendency to build it up, to throw around it a false glare, to deceive men and ruin them for time and eternity, then all that can be said or done by men who do not profess religion. They are frequently its leading officers - its worshipful masters, high priests, grand chaplains, grand commanders, etc.

In accepting these offices and wearing these unscriptural and high sounding titles, they violate the commands of the Saviour and disgrace his cause. “If ye love me” said Jesus, “keep my commandments.” What are they? The following is one - “Be ye not called Rabbi!” that is, **master**. To receive and wear the title, master, is a violation of a plain command from Christ. Those professed Christians and ministers who belong to the lodge, many times accept and wear this title with the addition **worshipful**. Worshipful master is the name by which they are known among the craft. Is not this profane as well as a violation of a positive command? Is it not assuming a title which belongs to none but God? Are creatures - professors of the Christian religion, to be worshipped? How do ministers of Christ, pastors and Sunday school teachers, appear in midnight assemblies of their fellow men, under the title **worshipful master**? Can they pretend for a moment that their divine Master approves this? The sinful nature of this title almost disappears, when we consider the nature of other titles which are accepted and worn by the same class of church members. What authority have they for assuming and wearing the title, high priest, or grand high priest? "No man," says the great apostle, "taketh this honour unto himself, (to be called a high priest,) but he that is called of God as was Aaron." On what possible ground can Christians pretend to justify themselves in wearing this title? Are they called of God to be high priests and grand high priests? They tread on forbidden ground - a positive command from God lies before them to which they appear to pay no regard; else, why do they violate it? They have no more authority for assuming this title under the present dispensation, than private members of the Jewish nation had under that dispensation. Will anyone pretend that members of that nation who had no connection with the priest's office, would have been justifiable in assuming this title and wearing the robes of Aaron? Read Numbers 26:9-10, and there witness the destruction of Korah and his company, and the fire of God's wrath which consumed the two hundred and fifty princes, merely because they aspired to his office when it did not belong to them! Is the thing any less sinful now than it was then? Away with these abominations from the house of God. We have no "grand high priests," nor "grand commanders," nor "sovereigns of sovereigns," nor "knights of the Holy Ghost." No, we are **"all brethren"**; and have all **"one Master"**, and the greatest among us wear no higher title than **"servant"** - Matthew 23:7-11.

The sublime honors which the institution confers on professors of Christianity, are the corrupt and bewitching honors of the world; such as Christians should look upon with the utmost contempt. Will Christians who profess to seek a heavenly country - a city which hath foundations, whose builder and maker is God; will they so lower themselves as to be running after these worldly honors, and playing with these empty baubles?

All this abomination - this system of self-righteousness, of impiety and mockery, of blasphemy, with its worldly honors and profane titles, is fellowshipped by Christian churches. Shall churches continue to follow this iniquity, or shall they separate from it? One or the other the Lord requires. There are many who believe that masonry is an evil and ought not to be fellowshipped, but take no active part against it. They are very inconsistent; for, if masonry is an evil and ought not to be fellowshipped, then it is the duty of every person to come up to the help of the Lord against it; to use all possible, prudent and justifiable means to remove it. The more a person can do, the more he is bound to do - the more the Lord requires of him, and the greater will be his criminality in neglecting to do it. There are others who not only withhold their aid to expose masonry, but extend all the influence they have to produce as much silence as possible on this subject. These brethren may sincerely believe that such a course is wisely adapted to do good; but they are surely "healing slightly the hurt of God's people." If they can succeed in keeping peace for a season, as some of them do, they have only healed the surface of the wound, while it remains to be probed to the bottom. Masonry will never be separated from the church without a struggle.

Nothing is more evident than that God is loudly calling upon Zion to arise and purify herself from the abominations. This can be attested to by the fact that in the last few years several good books have been written exposing this modern day paganistic cult for what it truly is, and some of these books have been written by 33rd degree masons. Here are a few good examples: **"Freemasonry: The Invisible Cult In Our Midst"**, written by a former worshipful master, Jack Harris, and **"The Deadly Deception"**, written by Jim Shaw, one of its top leaders, who was a 33rd degree mason, Knight Commander of the Court of Honor, Past Worshipful Master of a Blue Lodge, and Past Master of all Scottish Rite bodies. The other two books that I would like to make mention of are, **"Should a Christian be a Mason"**, by E.M. Storms and **"Christianity and American Freemasonry"**, by William J. Whalen. I believe that these four books have been greatly used to expose the evils of freemasonry in this present day.

Many think it is not best for churches to renounce masonry entirely - it will produce such an unhappy division and so much distress. But we must either go along with this abomination in the church, or separate from it. What shall we do? Which will agree with the purity of the gospel? A distressing scene would follow! Is this an evidence that we ought not to separate from that institution - that we ought to fellowship that which the bible pointedly condemns? Let me give you a good example from the bible that will illustrate the point I am trying to make. In Ezra, chapters nine and ten, we read of a difficult separation. At the time the Jews were carried away captive to Babylon, quite a number violated the commands of God by marrying heathen wives. This was discovered soon after their return from captivity, what was to be done? Here were more than one hundred, some of them priests and Levites - first men in the nation, who have fallen into sin. Must they separate from their wives and children? Must their families be broken up? What a distressing time! What an unhappy division! But iniquity was there. A command of God had been violated - a union formed which he had expressly forbidden: A separation must take place; the union must be dissolved, though it should part the dearest ties ever formed in nature. Husbands and wives, parents and children, must part; more than one hundred families must be broken up. If the people of God at the present day, have formed a connection which the scriptures forbid, they must dissolve it, let the consequences be ever so distressing. Should it annihilate whole churches, it would in no sense lessen the duty. Churches which are not formed according to the pattern of the new testament, are of little worth to the saviour. The glory of his kingdom does not consist in numbers, but in the purity of those who compose it.

It is taken for granted by many, that let masonry alone and it will eventually go into disrepute. These persons are greatly mistaken. They certainly are not acquainted with the nature of the system, and one would think they aren't with the nature of the human heart. Was it ever known that Satan gave up one of his strongholds peaceably, without a struggle to retain it, until compelled to by those weapons which are mighty through God? If the institution of masonry is not one of his strongly fortified castles, then he never had one on earth; and should he resign it peaceably, it would be something new. Christians who have joined the lodge, have something more to do than merely to say, that they will not attend lodge meetings anymore. They have done wrong - have committed a great evil. They must confess and utterly renounce this evil. Nothing less than a humble, penitent confession, and complete renunciation, will ever restore them to the fellowship and communion of the church of God. Every sincere follower of Jesus Christ who has been duped by masonry, will, when he sees his wrong, cheerfully, and with a broken heart, take this step.

Look at the numerous profane temples of masonry scattered over the face of the land! How many lodges and chapters in every state? A grand lodge, a grand royal arch chapter, a grand encampment of knights of each state. Have these numerous and powerful grand bodies fallen into disrepute? Will they without the most vigilant exertions on the part of the people? There is much to be done; and a great share of it must be done by the churches. Our work must be thoroughly done - the harmful plant must not only be broken down, but dug up, and its roots **"exposed to the scorching rays of the sun"**.

Masonry will by no means die of itself; nor will it separate itself from the church of God. No: it will cling to it, like the deadly **scorpion** to the victim on which it fastens. The church must therefore separate from it. When Ezra, the Jewish priest, discovered the sin unto which some of his brethren had fallen by marrying heathen wives, had he delayed a separation under the great mistake, that they would eventually see their wrong, separate themselves and the evil die away, what would have been the consequences? Would not those who had joined affinity with the heathens, have clung to them until the day of their death? Would not others have followed their example and have committed the same sin? When the evil was discovered, then was the time to apply the remedy. Had it been delayed, the danger would have increased. So it is with masonry; every person who has joined that heathenish institution, though he may feel as strongly attached to it as the Jews did to their heathen wives, is required by the bible to dissolve it immediately. When the people of God, in the days of Martin Luther, began to discover the polluted doctrine and character of the church of Rome, what was their duty? Was it still to maintain a connection with it - let popery alone - let it die away? Did they not here the voice of God through the scriptures, saying "Come out of her, my people, that ye be not partakers of her sins, and that ye receive not of her plagues"? Those who did not obey this command, were partakers of her sins, and consequently received of her plagues. Those who will not separate from masonry, are partakers of the sins of the institution, and likewise will receive of the plagues of God.

A separation from masonry, is urged by the plain commands of the new testament. 2 Cor. 6:14-17 *"Be ye not unequally yoked together with unbelievers: for what fellowship hath righteousness with unrighteousness? And what communion hath light with darkness? And what concord hath Christ with Belial? Or what part hath the temple of God with idols: for ye are the temple of the living God; as God hath said, I will dwell in them, and walk in them; and I will be their God, and they shall be my people. Wherefore come out from among them, and be ye separate, saith the Lord, and touch not the unclean thing; and I will receive you."*

There is no fellowship, no communion, no concord, no agreement, between the church of our Lord Jesus Christ, and the corrupt institution of freemasonry. Masonry is that which the gospel condemns: It is an "unclean thing". Christians are therefore to separate themselves from it.

Again - *"And have no fellowship with the unfruitful works of darkness, but rather reprove them. For it is a shame even to speak of those things which are done of them in secret."* Perhaps no system ever existed, which is more strikingly characterized as works of darkness, than masonry. Even they are ashamed to speak of the things which are done of them in secret. With these unfruitful works of darkness - these shameful secrets, Christians are to have no fellowship: and they have something more to do then merely to disfellowship them - *"But reprove them"*. Eph. 5:11-12. Also 2 Thess. 3:6 says - *"Now we command you, brethren, in the name of our Lord Jesus Christ, that ye withdraw yourselves from any brother that walketh disorderly, and not after the tradition which he received of us."*

Is it not disorderly to join that institution, to adhere to it, to take its unchristian and unconstitutional oaths, to practice its profane and mock ceremonies? If not, pray tell us what would be disorderly. If we are not to fellowship all this in the church of God, what shall we not fellowship there? These passages of scripture make our duty plain - so plain that the wayfaring man though a fool need not err therein. It is time that the church spoke out against this evil, and even though the minister or Sunday school teacher may receive the scoffs of the world, and the censures of some of their brethren; they can show the most unequivocal testimony of the holy scriptures - a **" thus saith the Lord"**, for what they do, and certainly **"we ought to obey God rather than men"**.

It is of the utmost importance, however, that every move on the subject, should be dictated by the mild spirit of the Saviour. An intemperate spirit, harsh and hasty measures, tend directly to defeat the object designed to be accomplished. "A soft answer turneth away wrath, but grievous words stir up strife." "And the servant of the Lord must not strive, but be gentle unto all men, apt to teach, patient, in meekness instructing those that oppose themselves, if God peradventure will give them repentance to the acknowledging of the truth." "Be ye therefore wise as serpents and harmless as doves." Perhaps there never was a time in which this dove-like spirit was more needed among churches than at the present. Amidst the turmoil and confusion which exist in many places, it highly becomes the Christian soldier to be calm - to keep in his mind the precious words of the wise man - "He that is slow to anger is better than the mighty; and he that ruleth his spirit, than he that taketh a city." We should "contend earnestly for the faith," yet in **"meekness"**; we should be "steadfast, unmovable" in our course, yet "gentle". Churches cannot be too much guarded against measures which may tend rather to divide, than reclaim those who have sinned. *"But ye, beloved, building up yourselves on your most holy faith, praying in the Holy Ghost, keep yourselves in the love of God, looking for the mercy of Our Lord Jesus Christ unto eternal life. And of some have compassion, making a difference; and others save with fear, pulling them out of the fire; hating even the garments spotted by the flesh. Now unto him that is able to keep you from falling, and to present you faultless before the presence of his glory, with exceeding joy, to the only wise God our Saviour, be glory and majesty, dominion and power, both now and forever. Amen."* Jude 20-25.

Chapter 13

ON THE INFLUENCE OF MINISTERS

People generally, are disposed to put too much confidence in ministers of the gospel. If a minister appears to be devotional, if he prays and preaches with a degree of energy, and his ministry seems successful, it is not uncommon for people to suppose that he is almost infallible. It is extremely difficult, in many cases, to convince them that such a man can be wrong. They don't seem to realize, that ministers spring from the same polluted root as themselves, and are equally liable to embrace error and fall into sin, as they are. Nor, perhaps, are they aware of the solemn and painful truth, that professed ministers of the gospel have done more than any other group of men on earth, to corrupt the church of God. Two of the top T.V. Evangelist are good examples, one is serving 45 years in a federal penitentiary, and the other was defrocked by the Assemblies of God. These ministers were placed at the avenues of the church to resist error; and when error and sin sent forth its polluted streams into the church, they have, in some instances, opened the flood gates themselves. All the errors which were ever brought into the church, and all the corruptions which have for ages tarnished the glory of the kingdom, have been the device of some clergyman or ecclesiastical council. And it is by the authority and influence of the same class of men, that these errors and corruptions are spread extensively and maintained. If it were not for their influence, thousands of the saints of God, would renounce their errors, and embrace and practice the truth as it is revealed in the bible. All the "filthiness and abominations" of the church of Rome, were introduced by the **clergy**. Those who have been esteemed as good men, have persecuted even unto death, those who have differed from them in opinion. Are ministers more holy now than they have been in the past?

How many ministers have seemed to give great evidence of piety, their efforts have been wonderfully blessed of God, yet they have turned out to be wicked men. I personally know of three church of God ministers in my area, who have lost their churches and resigned their ministry, because of adultery and sins of the flesh. One of the ministers held his pastorate for 20 years, and the other two held theirs for 10 years each. Were these men right because they appeared to be pious, and their labors blessed? No! God blessed them, not because they deserved to be blessed; but for the sake of his Son and the many who were lost. If ministers preach and pray like angels from heaven - if a swelling tide of success follows them to the grave, these things are no sure evidence that what they do is right, or that they are God's ministers. We must not take for granted, that what the most devotional, understanding and useful ministers do, is right; we must test it by the same rule we do our own conduct, or the conduct of others, and judge for ourselves. It is not some preacher, but the word of God, that should be the standard, by which we measure our lives.

I believe that ministers, have done more than any other group of men, to introduce masonry into the church. In the last fifteen years I have had two pastors who were masons, my children's Sunday school teacher was a mason, and a friend of mine in the ministry just joined the lodge about three months ago. Also I know of three other ministers in the church of God who are masons, not to mention the several members of the various congregations who belong to the lodge - then we set back and wonder why the church is weak, powerless and losing ground. Yes, it is sad to say, but ministers have been leaders in these things. They have joined the institution, have recommended it as a **"good thing,"** and have even praised it as **"divine."** Their brethren have supposed, that it must be what they have recommended it to be, and have fallen into the same sin. How many have they, by their example and influence, lured into those secret chambers; many of whom, no doubt, will go down to perdition, under the guilt of Masonic oaths! Had these ministers stood where they ought to have stood, as pillars in the house of God - had they kept clear from this unscriptural union - had they borne testimony against these unfruitful works of darkness, and these shameful secrets; masonry could never have found its way into the church - the door would have been effectually closed against it. But they have opened the door, and have helped in the evil with their own hands; and many of them appear determined that it shall not be removed.

It is high time that people were awake - that churches should see that those ministers who are masons, however high they may stand, can err; have and do still err, on this subject. What a wound have these men inflicted upon the precious cause of the Saviour! What a reproach they have brought upon the ministry! Great confidence, as I have said, is often put in ministers. They are looked up to as examples - and indeed they should be. Men of no religion, often suppose that what ministers do and say, is right; But when they see these ministers leave the path of the just, violate the laws of Christ, and do that which they themselves would not do, what a stumbling block does it cast before them. Irreligious men - even the open enemies of Christianity can judge for themselves, that the conduct of those ministers who belong to the Masonic lodge, and are maintaining their connection with it, is highly unbecoming their profession; and indeed a disgrace to it. What a weapon they have put into the hands of such men! How much occasion have they given them to say, Christianity is a fable, and those who profess it, even its ministers, are no better than others - than ourselves! The only course these ministers can take, which will do away with the disgrace they have already brought upon the cause; is to renounce, in the true spirit of the gospel, their connection with the institution, and confess their wrong. This, and nothing but this, will heal the wound, and restore them to their former standing before God.

To those who may take an unjustifiable occasion, from the conduct of these men, I would observe, that it has no bearing against the Christian religion. It perfectly corresponds with the history of the human heart, from the foundation of the world, as given in the bible. These men have done, just as the bible informs us others, even those who professed to be good men, have done before them. Their conduct must testify, not against Christianity, but against themselves - against their **personal piety**. There was a Judas among the first ministers of Christ.

Why is it that so many men of influence who are not masons, keep in the background, and not let it be known on which side they stand? If these men would come forward and show themselves on the Lord's side, as they are bound to by all that is dear in Zion, the struggle would soon be over. Are these men afraid of losing their good name, their popular influence among masons? Is this the reason why they will not oppose what they know and acknowledge to be an abomination? Perhaps they have been told, and sincerely believe, that should they oppose the institution, it would be a serious injury to their reputation. Does the Lord require his people to pursue a course which would secure the friendship of the lodge? Is it wrong for them to do anything which will stir up their wrath, and provoke them to kindle the fires of persecution? "Woe unto you," says the Saviour, "when all good men speak well of you, for so did their fathers of the false prophets."

There are many professors of Christianity, who, in a time of peace, when things are going good, when all that shines is taken for gold, are much admired; but do they make good soldiers in a time of war? Will they stand by the cross of Christ in the dark and cloudy day, and contend for the truth, at the risk of popularity, interest, and life itself? Look at the course which many ministers have pursued on masonry. Do they think it imprudent to take an active part against that which they have so frequently denounced as corrupt? Or is there, in their view, something to be lost now?

Have ministers of God anything to lose? If they have, let them relinquish their hold of it. If they have anything but the precious cause of their divine Master, let them cast it away, it is only a dead weight. If they have a name or a character which can be destroyed, let it go; it is certainly worth nothing. Those who sustain the Christian character, and pursue the oath of Christian duty, and with the great apostle to the Gentiles, have **suffered the loss of all things that they may win Christ,** have nothing to lose - nor have they anything to gain, but Christ. But when we see men clinging to their popularity, refusing to come out boldly in defence of what they know to be the truth, for fear they will lose something, what unfavorable conclusion must we draw? There is too much seeking to save life among professed Christians. "He that seeketh to save his life shall lose it", says the Saviour. Christians should not fear to have "their names cast out as evil, for the son of man's sake." How many twists and turns must those individuals make, who seek to save their lives! yet, after all their carefulness, must lose them.

There are many who seem to consider it a disgrace to suffer the reproach and slander of men, for opposing that anti-Christian system. But what does Jesus say? **"Blessed are ye when men shall revile you, and persecute you, and shall say all manner of evil against you falsely, for my sake."** If a man, from pure motives, labors to expose masonry, and is reviled, persecuted, and all manner of evil spoken against him falsely - if in strict accordance with the blasphemous oath of illustrious knights, he is pointed out to the world by their malicious tongues as an **"unworthy and vicious vagabond"**, it is so far from being a disgrace, that it is an honor, and the greatest honor which the enemies of God can confer upon him. Those who suffer this persecution, will perhaps, enjoy peace of conscience, and the approval of Almighty God, in as great a degree, as those who, to maintain their popular course, to save their lives and avoid this persecution, have neglected their duty and sacrificed the interest of Zion.

It is true that a man who takes a decided stand against the Masonic lodge, is often treated with the greatest abuse. A war of "VENGEANCE" is proclaimed against him. He may depend on it, that his character will be thoroughly tried, and if it is not good, it will be publicly known. Masons have always held out the dreadful idea, that a man who should oppose them, would suffer the loss of character and influence. What abuse they have dealt out to those who have attempted to expose their system! What can be their object! A very plain one - **to prevent the influence of truth.**

But why should it be considered a disgrace to any man to oppose masonry - to write and publish against it? Is the subject itself so vile as to disgrace a person who attempts to investigate it? If so, how contemptible must those appear, who enlist all their talents and influence in supporting it - who receive its honors and wear its titles! Look at the men, high in rank in both church and state, who are said to have patronized the institution, and to have been its grand dignitaries! Some of these have written and published volumes - have travelled from lodge to lodge, from chapter to chapter, and from one country to another, to advance the interest of the fraternity. They have freely expressed their views, and have labored to promote them. Now, is it wrong for a man to express his views fairly on the same subject? Even if they are not correct, yet if he advances them with a degree of fairness, why should he subject himself to the anger and abuse, of almost every member of the order? Why do they not meet him like men - in a fair exchange of arguments? And if his arguments are not good, expose them and put them down. If their cause is a good one, don't they have enough talent enlisted to support it, to defend it on this ground, by giving every opponent fair play? It may always be taken for granted, that a cause which cannot be defended in this way, had better be given up; it is poor, and cannot be the cause of truth. But this is a mode of warfare to which the brotherhood are not accustomed. Their cause cannot be supported by truth. It has ever been, and is to this day, supported and defended by falsehood and slander. Their strongest hold, is nothing less than a refuge of lies. Let them abandon this, and attempt to stand upon the ground of truth, and they cannot find one inch of such ground before them. Let the champions of masonry take this ground in its defence, instead of slandering the character of those, who have fairly shown that it is not founded in truth. This would be much more **"honorable"** than the course which they usually pursue.

Many churches today will not oppose masonry - instead, they are seeking peace with the institution. They are, therefore, unfavorably disposed toward every move which is calculated to disturb this peace. They are saying, "peace, peace, when there is no peace." There can be no peace between the cause of Christ and the cause of masonry. Unless righteousness can fellowship unrighteousness, light commune with darkness, Christ have concord with Belial, and there be an agreement between the temple of God and idols, there never can be peace between the church of God and the Masonic lodge. The only ground on which men can expect peace with masonry is, not to oppose it - let it alone - say nothing about it. Many of them, no doubt, would be willing to enter into a solemn covenant with the institution, never to oppose it. I ask these men to look at the terms on which they are so urgent for peace! Are they righteous? Will peace established on these terms be durable? Will the Lord own and bless it? On the same terms they may enjoy peace with all the cults and powers of darkness. But you cannot compromise to bring about peace and still do that which is pleasing in the eyes of the Lord. Christians are not to look for peace on this subject, until the last Masonic temple has been destroyed.

Christians are soldiers, and are commanded to "put on the whole armor of God," and to fight "against principalities, against powers, against the rulers of the darkness of this world, against spiritual wickedness in high places," and are "exhorted," that they "should earnestly contend for the faith which was once delivered unto the saints." Are they at liberty to compromise with any of these enemies who would destroy this faith? If they may with one, they may with all; then they may lay aside the armor; they can have no further use for it. Armor is of no use in time of peace. But it is never a time of peace with saints of God in this life; and if they even propose to make peace with anything which is unholy, they cast the greatest dishonor upon Him who has chosen them to be soldiers. They should always have on their whole armor, every part of it, and always be advancing the war upon the kingdom of darkness. They are to make war with the false systems, which are invented by "principalities," by "powers," and by "the rulers of the darkness of this world." Every false system of religion, is designed to undermine the gospel of Christ, and to overthrow his cause. Masonry is such a system; and if the saints are justifiable not to oppose it, they are equally justifiable not to oppose any system Satan ever invented. Then, where would be the faith which was once delivered to them? Would they in this way preserve it pure and unadulterated as they received it from heaven? What invention of Satan's can be more dangerous to the cause of Christ, than one which claims kindred with it - to be the same in substance with it - or even to be a hand-maid to it? It is a thousand times more dangerous than one which professes open war.

It is true, that Christians are to be **"peace makers"**. But they should never even think of making peace with that which is at war with Christ and his kingdom. Though the gospel which they profess is the gospel of peace, yet it is the nature and design of it to produce war - war with the enemies of truth. Wherever this is preached in its purity, this war is carried on. It separates the dearest friends, sets them at variance, excites the most deadly hostility, which often terminates in the shedding of blood and the taking of life, by those who hate the truth. The Saviour, therefore, says, "Think not that I am come to send peace on earth; I came not to send peace, but a sword. For I have come to set a man at variance against his father, and the daughter against her mother, and the daughter-in-law against her mother-in-law. And a man's foes shall be they of his own household".

On this very ground, thousands are opposed to every move which is made against the Masonic lodge - they claim it causes division and hard feelings - it excites wrath. On this ground, too, books written against the institution have been condemned and their authors slandered. Do they not know, that books could not be published, exposing the iniquity of the lodge, without producing war? Because these books sow discord among churches and separate friends, is no proof that they ought to be condemned or that they do not contain important truth - or that they were not called into existence by the special providence of God. And if exposing masonry and contending against it, should create the most unpleasant strife, in families and churches - should it fling wide open the gates of hell, and provoke the adversary to muster all his legions - should thousands of the dear saints of God, be persecuted even unto death, it would furnish no evidence that masonry is right, or that we ought to be at peace with it. But what is the object to be gained in being at peace with the lodge? Is it not this, in many instances - monetary assistance? Are there not many who profess to be ministers of Christ, who have joined the lodge, taken its profane oaths, bound themselves under its horrid curses, for no other purpose than to obtain more liberal support in the ministry? Are they not still clinging to it for the same reason? If they were to renounce this unscriptural connection, they would not only be pursued with the tongue of slander, but many of them, no doubt, would suffer the consequences, in a pecuniary respect. Their benevolent brethren might "oppose their interest and disturb their business", and reduce them to want. On the other hand, there are many ministers who are not masons, and who sincerely believe that masonry is an evil, yet are at peace with it, principally because they fear the loss of friends and support. Perhaps some of their members belong to the fraternity, and should they come out and oppose it, many of the streams by which their temporary wants have been supplied, would be cut off, and they reduced to the necessity of trusting in the providence of God for their daily bread. Which is worth the most to the cause of Christ - a few dollars and cents, or the eternal truths of the bible? Put your finger upon a solitary truth in the whole bible, which you would part with for thirty, or twice thirty, or ten times thirty pieces of silver! Are Christians to pursue that course with masonry, or with any other corrupt institution in existence, by which they may obtain the most money from it? "God forbid."

But what would be the consequences as to these several institutions, should masonry be disfellowshipped by churches? This is a question which is entirely beyond the reach of any human being to answer; and it is one with which we have nothing to do. This is the question which interest us - **Is Masonry corrupt?** This is not determined by the quantity of money we can obtain from members of that society, to aid in the cause of Christ; but by an investigation of its principles, oaths, ceremonies, writings and practices. If on such an investigation, the lodge should appear to be anti-Christian, every person's duty is plain - to withdraw from it - to disfellowship it - and to devote his talents, however feeble or mighty, to its overthrow, regardless of consequences - God has promised to take care of us.

Have not Christians read, that "the silver and the gold, and the cattle upon a thousand hills," belong to the Lord of hosts? Do they not know that he will bring these treasures into the church as fast as they are needed? There can be no necessity, then, of making peace with the world, for the sake of getting their money. Does the kingdom of Christ lean for support on the kingdom of darkness? Does he solicit the aid of that kingdom? By no means. He is the independent Jehovah, and is able to sustain his own cause without the aid of his enemies! If he wishes to make use of the gold and silver, which he has put into their hands, he will do it; but never, never, by making peace with their corrupt inventions, which are designed to overthrow his cause and to rob him of his glory . The idea into which many have fallen, at the present day, of courting the favor and friendship of wicked men, and of the kingdoms of this world, to aid in supporting benevolent institutions, or in promoting the cause of the Redeemer, is going far away from the examples of the new testament.

For ministers and Christians to join the Masonic lodge, for the purpose of being more popular, and of getting more money, is insulting the Saviour. For others who are not masons, to be at peace with it for the purpose of obtaining the same ends, is equally blamable. "It is better to trust the Lord than to put confidence in princes." "Cursed be the man that trusteth in man, and maketh flesh his arm."

Chapter 14

INDEPENDENCE OF THE MIND

As to the independence of the human mind, all men stand on the same level. It is what all have received from Him, in whom they live, and move, and have their being. All have equal liberty to think, to reason, and to investigate for themselves.

This liberty of mind is essential to man's salvation. If he may not freely and fairly investigate any moral or religious subject which may be presented, or is under obligation to embrace it without examining it, then he is in the utmost danger of being like the man who built his house upon the sand; the rain descended, the floods came, the winds blew and beat upon it, and it fell, and great was the fall of it. How many thousands have been ruined in this way! who, though they have not taken the sacrilegious oaths of masonry, yet by a corrupt and tyrannical priesthood, have been denied the privilege of examining the Christian faith for themselves; and have been induced, and even compelled to embrace a faith suited to the views of its authors

How many, too, have been ruined in the same way by masonry? Those whom they considered great and good men, have told them, that masonry is the same in substance with Christianity: without examining it, they have embraced it as such, as their religion; have rested their eternal hopes upon it, and have died in the full belief that it is a saving system.

Also, this liberty is essential to the purity of the church of God. If its members may not freely investigate every moral or religious sentiment, and renounce and disfellowship as in their judgment the rules of the gospel shall dictate, then the door is open for the introduction of every type of error, which will soon corrupt both their faith and practice. Look at the abominations of the church of Rome! These false doctrines, such as, celibacy, transubstantiation, purgatory, infant baptism, invoking saints, assumption of Mary, etc., etc., being sanctioned by a polluted priesthood, have been imposed on the gullible, and they, not being permitted to examine for themselves, have embraced them and have become blindly attached to them.

Equally essential is this liberty to the purity of democratic institutions. If the people may not freely discuss any point whatever, which stands connected with their civil or political freedom, if their voice may not be heard on all such subjects, then their free institutions, of which they may proudly boast, are in the utmost danger of being corrupted, undermined and overthrown. To deprive a people of this liberty, is the high road to tyranny and despotism.

I will now show the reader, that it is the nature and obvious design of the Masonic institution, to tyrannize over the human mind, and to rob it of this freedom. In the first oath which is administered, the candidate is made to swear, in the most solemn manner, and to bind himself under no less penalty than to have his throat cut, his tongue torn out, etc., that he "will always hail freemasonry - that he will not write, print, stamp, stain, hew, cut, carve, indent, paint, or engrave it, on anything moveable or immovable, under the whole canopy of heaven. "O sacrilegious oath! Thus the deluded votary of masonry, on the very threshold of the institution, is induced to swear away, not only his life, but what is worth a thousand times more, the liberty of freely exercising the powers of the mind,

By swearing that he will always hail masonry, supposes, first - that he embraces the whole system, without knowing, by a fair investigation, what it is. This oath is administered before the mysteries of masonry are communicated to him; consequently, at the time he solemnly swears that he will always hail them and never reveal them, he is perfectly ignorant of them. Now if it is right for men to embrace masonry, without investigating it for themselves, so far as to know what it is, then it is equally right for them to embrace any article of faith, or any system, whether religious, philosophical, or political, without investigating it, to know what it is. This sentiment is the foundation on which the boasted Masonic fabric has rested for ages. Introduce it into the church. Let it be a law there, as it is in the lodge, that every member shall embrace, and solemnly covenant that he will always hail the church's doctrinal beliefs without knowing what they are - without examining a solitary one of them. Such a law may with as much propriety exist in the church, as in any other society. But what would be the consequences? They would soon be seen in the superstition, bigotry, enthusiasm, corruptions and abominations of the church, and in the ruin of souls. This is the doctrine of Mahomet, improved on by the pope. The idea supposes, secondly - that the candidate is never at liberty to investigate masonry with a view to know whether it ought to be hailed or not. He not only embraces it without a fair, or even a superficial investigation, but swears, in essence, that he never will investigate it. If the oath supposes, that he is at liberty to investigate the system, with a view to know whether it ought to be hailed or not, it also supposes, that after such an investigation, he may come to the conclusion not to hail it; whereas he solemnly swears without any reserve or condition whatever, that he will always hail it. Carry out this sentiment. If a man may in one instance be prohibited the privilege of examining a subject, a professed system of morality or religion, he may in another, and indeed in every instance; and thus be effectually deprived of that liberty of mind, which is essential to the end to which he exists. Here is one instance in which he is deprived of it by arbitrary law, and the principle by which it is done, in this one instance, might with equal propriety do it in every instance.

Again - that the candidate should be bound not to reveal any art or arts, part or parts, point or points of masonry; not to write nor print it, etc., supposes, that he must not in any circumstances whatever, communicate a solitary idea for the information of others. In the obligation of illustrious knights, the candidate is bound in still stronger terms, if possible. He swears, that "to the end of life," he will not either "with good or bad design, ever take the least step, or measure, or be instrumental in any such object, to betray" the secrets of the degree - that he "will never speak on or upon, or breathe, high or low, any ceremonies or secrets, whereby any opinion, even of the nature and general principles of the institution can be found by any other person, be he a mason or otherwise, than a true knight companion of the cross." Let the knowledge which he may possess of the institution be what it may, ever so interesting to others, tending in its nature to promote their happiness in the highest degree, both in this life and that which is to come; or if he knows that the institution is ever so corrupt - that it sanctions the greatest wickedness - that it is designed to disorganize every system of social happiness, yet he must not reveal it, nor write, nor print one syllable of it, nor the bare resemblance of a syllable of it - must not speak on or upon, breathe high or low, anything by which this may be known, on peril of having his throat cut, his tongue torn out, or of dying the infamous death of a traitor, and of suffering the eternal torments of hell.

It is understood, that the members of the fraternity are at liberty to speak in its favor, if they do not disclose its secrets and mysteries; but under no circumstances whatever, to the end of life, are they at liberty to speak against it, though they may possess the clearest convictions of its inward depravity. This is plain, not only from the above oaths, but from their manner of dealing with those of their members, who dare to be free men; to cast off the Masonic yoke; to speak, write and publish their views of the institution. They are not only expelled, (which is by no means a disgrace, though designed to be), but are pursued with that kind of mean, abusive treatment, which is well befitting the fallen spirits of another world. Masonic vengeance, without justice, is meted out to them.

From the foregoing remarks, we may account for the extreme ignorance of the grand majority of the members of that institution, and of people generally on this subject. The more "knowing ones" of the order, have been determined, and have used every precaution, to prevent a free and fair investigation of the moral nature and tendency of the system. People must believe it to be just what they freely assert it to be, without so much as looking at it for themselves. This, thousands have done, those who are masons and those who are not. The members of the institution, who in reality become the dupes of this imposition, who hail masonry without knowing by an impartial examination whether it ought to be hailed, are more or less, under the influence of bigotry and fanaticism. They have not reasoned themselves on the subject, and of course reason, in their view, has nothing to do with it. They will not hear to reason; nor will they enter into a fair debate on the subject. Many of them will not even read a book written against the institution, though written ever so fairly. All such books are rejected, and their authors doomed to destruction, "whether they be right or wrong." With such men it is perfectly useless to attempt to reason. They are blind and deaf. They are thorough proof against the fairest and most convincing arguments.

There are hundreds of masons, who are, and ever have been, perfectly ignorant of the true spirit of the institution. Though they tacitly acknowledge that the oaths which have been made public, are in substance correct; yet they are under such a strong delusion, that they cannot or will not be made to see, that these oaths are repugnant to the principles of good government and the Christian religion. They defend the lodge, adhere to it - and sincerely believe, at least appear to, that it is a "good thing;" though disgraced by the conduct of bad members, as is the case with every society. On other subjects these men will talk with candor. But the fact is, they have never examined masonry; they have taken it for granted - have embraced it in the dark;

perfectly so, in every sense of the word - have never come to the light to look at it. Such men, if they only knew it, are the mere tools of the order. But every honest mason, who fearlessly pulls the bandage from his eyes, and looks at the monster in the clear light of truth, steps back with abhorrence!

I can't understand why there is such an indifference on this subject in the churches. It surprises me that such a society should exist so long in America; that people should not see their danger, until aroused by the overthrow of law, liberty, and religion and by a tremendous shaking of their freedom.

The notion of a secret society, a society which is not known in law, which usually convenes in the dark, conceals its principles and practices from the public, whatever pretensions it shall make, ought to excite alarm in the breasts of all honest men. Must a society which has for its grand and exclusive object, "universal charity," be a secret one? There must be some selfish, some ambitious, if not wicked design, covered beneath the mantle of its secrecy and its false pretences. What do good men, acting from good motives, wish to do in secret, guarded by "the tyler's sword?" I answer, nothing! The very idea of professors of Christianity belonging to a secret society, is, of itself, a sufficient reason why they ought not at the same time to belong to the visible church of God. The false glare, the deceitful outside of the institution, and the idea which has been so strongly planted in the public mind, that masonry must not be freely and fairly investigated, have prevented people from seeing the subject at an earlier day, in this light.

Masonry, in denying its members the liberty to speak, write, and publish what they please, on any subject they please, to be accountable only to the laws of God and their country, in prohibiting this free exercise of the mind by arbitrary laws, which are enforced by the most barbarous penalties, presents a powerful reason why it ought to be abolished. A man who is influenced by the holy precepts of the Christian religion, or even nothing more than a love of national liberty, cannot understandingly, support this organized system of tyranny.

What is more debasing and demoralizing than the bondage of the mind! Individuals, who basely yield their mental independence, and embrace sentiments and systems, which they have not investigated, and of which they know nothing only by hearsay, are, so far as they submit to this imposition, blind, ignorant, bigoted zealots. How many are there, who seldom pretend to reason on any subject, unless it concerns their sordid interest. Strictly speaking, they "pin their faith on other men's sleeves." They have their particular friends in whom they confide; and what these friends tell them, is "law and gospel," without the shadow of a doubt - beyond all controversy. The only step they take in a course of reasoning, (if it may be called reasoning) is, our friends say it is so - it is therefore true - we believe it. Just so far, and no further, do thousands reason on the subject of masonry. A minister, a professed Christian, a father, a son, or some other relative, whom they respect, has told them that masonry is "a good thing," and they believe it, and perhaps at the same time will acknowledge, that they know nothing about it. How much more powerful is this kind of influence over the hearts of men, than the influence of truth!

Every man should resolve to be independent - to use the powers of mind which God has given him, in the fearless and diligent search of truth and duty. To think, examine, and judge for himself, on all subjects. To adopt no system, whether political, philosophical, or religious; of whatever school, or by whatever authority or great names it may be upheld, without a thorough and candid investigation. Anything short of this is beneath the dignity of man, and is a base prostitution of his noble nature.

Chapter 15

DUTIES OF THOSE WHO CONDUCT RELIGIOUS JOURNALS

I shall now speak on the freedom of the press. Who can estimate the influence which a free and well conducted press must have on the present and eternal happiness of a people! Every editor of a paper, radio announcer, or television producer, is emphatically "a public sentinel on the watch-tower of liberty." His responsibility is great - the duty which he owes God and his fellow men is great. No class of men, (ministers excepted), have a greater and more extensive influence over the human mind, and do more either to darken or enlighten it, than those who control the energies of the television and the press. It is their duty, not only to spread abroad the light of science and the glorious light of the blessed gospel, but especially to guard the civil and religious rights of the people; and fearless of all consequences, to wage an exterminating and eternal war with every enemy which threatens to attack these rights. Those who attempt to fill these highly responsible positions, ought to be men who are free from the influence of sordid motives; who have no interest other than the public good; whose veracity, self-denial, and integrity of soul, will never allow them to neglect their duty, or selfishly to betray the public interest, to further their own goals.

Will the principles of that "honorable" institution, freemasonry, allow editors of public newspapers and journals to possess these qualifications and to perform their duty? Suppose an editor has been hoodwinked and haltered in a Masonic lodge, and made to swear that he will always hail, ever conceal, and never reveal masonry - that he will never write nor print it, nor the mere resemblance of anything by which it may be known - that he will keep the secrets of a master mason, murder and treason excepted, and those of a royal arch mason, murder and treason not excepted; that he will extricate him from his difficulty, whether he be right or wrong; that he will promote his political preferment in opposition to another; that he will support the constitution of the grand lodge and of the grand royal arch chapter of his State, etc., etc. Put all these oaths together, and if he considers them binding, is he to be acknowledged as a public sentinel? In how many instances may he be induced to betray his trust, and to sacrifice the cause of the people to that of the grand lodge or grand royal arch chapter? Suppose an attempt should be made to disclose the secrets of the order, an editor was killed, and the printing offices burned to the ground, to cover the attempt? Suppose this royal arch editor, who was a friend of the one killed, should be acquainted with the whole affair, and should be warned by his royal arch companions to keep it a secret - not to print one word about it, on peril of having his "skull struck off and his brains exposed to the scorching rays of the sun." What course would he take? His duty would be plain, to expose the whole transaction as far as he had become acquainted with it - to sound the alarm in the ears of his countrymen. But would he do this? Indeed he would not, so long as he considered his Masonic oaths binding. He would pursue the same course which hundreds have pursued in the past - to prostitute the liberties of the press, to the infamous cause of arson and murder. Every Masonic editor throughout the country, who has considered his obligations binding, and has planned to defend the institution, has pursued this scandalous course.

No **honest** man can understandingly conduct a Masonic journal - a journal designed to defend the institution "through thick and thin." An honest man will tell the truth. But a man who intends to defend masonry, feels solemnly bound to conceal truth; to perplex, bewilder, and deceive. The more skillful he is in this depraved course, the better qualified he is to be a Masonic editor.

I thank the Lord today, for publishing houses, who dare, in the face of Masonic vengeance, to be free, and to speak out, in the cause of truth, liberty and virtue! Every American citizen, who truly appreciates the liberties he enjoys, will give thanks to Almighty God for this! If it were not for the freedom of the press, the Eagle of our country would soon speed her flight to some other region of the earth - our sun would soon go down in darkness - depend upon it, our nation would soon be engulfed in ruin! The free presses of these publication houses are worth a thousand times their weight in gold. But as we look at those who are free, we cannot help wondering, how many there are, lying prostrate at the shrine of masonry, whose editors have wickedly concealed or perverted truth - have labored to throw a midst before the eyes of the people, and have poured a torrent of high handed abuse upon those who have espoused the cause of God and freedom. Such editors are traitors, the worst of traitors to their country. They have merited, and will certainly receive, the everlasting abhorrence of a virtuous people - a people, whom they have grossly insulted, and whose dearest rights they have mocked; and if they do not repent, will meet the frowns of Him who sits in the heavens, and will "laugh at their calamity, and mock when their fear cometh." The Masonic lodge, in the past has warned some of the free-spirited editors, louder than in words, be silent on the infamous and bloody deeds of our ancient and honorable, and heaven-born institution, or we will break you right or wrong!

I personally receive at this time, seven church papers or religious journals, and only two of the seven have ever spoken out against the Masonic lodge or published anything against it. They are "The Sword of the Lord" published in Murfreesboro, Tennessee, and the "Reformation witness", published by the Church of God "pastors' fellowship, in Winchester, Kentucky. It amazes me, that in the midst of all the efforts which are made to evangelize the world, a system exists, which professes to be religious, and which mocks the Saviour, the hope of the Christian, and the very existence of the church: yet, those editors who profess to guard the purity of the church, to furnish her with a knowledge of the most interesting movements of the day, dare not investigate the claims of this organization. How many timid creatures there are, not only editors, but others, who, under the Masonic threat, pull off their hats and bow to the order, and would almost submit to the humiliation of kissing the great toe of some grand dignitary.

Objections have been raised against discussing masonry in a religious paper. But I ask, why should masonry not be discussed in a religious journal? It professes to be a religious institution. Can any sound reason be offered, why the claims of a religious, or even a moral institution, should not be fairly investigated in a religious paper? Is masonry such a contemptible thing as to disgrace the columns of such a paper? Masonry's hostility is no greater towards a religious paper, than towards a political one, should it write on this subject. An effort by them to close the columns of any paper, carries in it, an implied but not spoken acknowledgment, that their cause will not bear examination - else, why should they be unwilling to have it examined? Do they feel able to defend it? Are they satisfied that the public on a free investigation of it, will become convinced that it is, what it professes to be? If they were, would they not be the first to urge on such an investigation, in every religious or political paper in circulation? But an effort to prevent this, is, I repeat it, an unspoken acknowledgment that their cause is weak, and that a fair discussion would overthrow it.

What an amazing contrast there is, between the conduct of these apostles of masonry, and the conduct of our Lord Jesus Christ! His cause and his claims, are presented before the world - before all classes of men, for a fair investigation. All have the privilege, and all are commanded to examine for themselves, and no man is bound to believe in him without evidence. "Search the scriptures," says he; and again - "If I do not the works of my Father, believe me not." He did not require the Jews to believe in him as the promised Messiah, without presenting before them for their examination, such evidence as would establish the truth of his divine mission. His cause is not a secret one; it is open for the investigation of all. But here is a class of men, who profess to be followers of this same Jesus, to copy his examples, who have a cause which they say is the same in substance with his cause, yet are unwilling that one word should be spoken, written, or published about it, with the idea of looking into its nature.

That masonry ought not to be discussed in a paper, because it professes to be devoted to religion, is an objection of no weight. Here is the very place to investigate it, and the pens of Christian editors are the proper instruments by which it ought to be done. Masonry professes to be religious, has crept into the church, has produced, and is still producing trouble there. The question is, whether it ought to be fellowshipped, or disfellowshipped. This question is important to the church and stands intimately connected with its peace and prosperity. How will this question ever be decided, unless the subject can be fairly presented, that people may see and judge for themselves? What method can be better adapted to accomplish the desired end, than a candid investigation of masonry in a religious paper? Here, I say, is the very place to investigate it. What possible objection can be raised against it? The Pope was aware, that the free circulation of the bible would expose his iniquity, the weakness and even wickedness of his claims - so during the dark ages the bibles were chained to the pulpits and no one had access to them but the clergy. So also, the free discussion of masonry, in a religious journal, would expose the unchristian nature of the institution. This we have reason to believe, is the very thing which its advocates fear.

Many churches are extremely ignorant, and greatly lacking on information concerning the Masonic lodge. How much help might be given them, how much light might be scattered among them, by a religious publication, of which there are many at the present time, but the majority of whom, remain as silent as the grave on this subject. If editors of religious papers would come out and do their duty, lend a suitable portion of their columns every week or month to this subject, the conflict between masonry and the church of God would soon be at an end. But the timid course that some of these editors have taken, has prolonged this battle, and hindered the cause of truth and righteousness - but victory is no less sure - God's word will prevail, and deliverance will arise from some other source.

Another objection which is brought forth on this subject, is the loss of support. For what purpose is a religious publication established? Is it to make money? Or to advance the kingdom of God, by circulating truth? If the primary reason is to make money, then it must adopt such measures and pursue such a course, as will secure it the most money. Are our religious presses set up for this purpose? I hope not. Their primary object professes to be, the advancement of the cause of Zion. Money is but a secondary object. Now, to object to the discussion of masonry in religious papers because it will subject them to a loss of support, is losing sight entirely, of the grand principles on which they profess to stand. The question to be decided is, does the interest of Zion call for the circulation of such information? If it does, then our duty is plain; and the truth must not be sacrificed to gain the support of any man, or any group of men.

Would masons condemn a religious paper which should take this independent ground? Would they withdraw their support? Undoubtedly they would. And this furnishes another convincing reason, why that system of oppression and tyranny ought to be exposed. What! will professed Christians denounce an editor, a brother in the church, and withdraw support from him, and use their influence to break him down, because he enters into a candid and scriptural examination of their beliefs and practice! A cause which requires, or sanctions such a course, is, to say the least, a very weak one. Professedly good men ought to abandon it entirely.

If editors of religious journals would seriously and

impartially look at this subject a moment, they must be convinced of a great neglect on their part and that God will surely call them to an account. Only a few of the churches are beginning to see the light on masonry, and to separate from that institution; but to what editor of a religious paper, are any of them indebted for assistance? What a pity that many such journals should be awed into silence by the sneers, the scoffs, the frowns, and the vengeance of a secret, self-created society! To those few editors, who will not be coerced into bowing at the shrine of masonry, and are going forward in the present holy conflict, between Christ and Antichrist, between liberty and tyranny, I would say, be of good courage, fear not, "for the Lord God omnipotent reigneth." "In due season we shall reap if we faint not."

Chapter 16

THE IMPROPRIETY OF PRETENDING TO LEAVE FREEMASONRY WITHOUT RENOUNCING ITS OBLIGATIONS

There are many who profess to be opposed to masonry but their theory and practice are very distant. They say that masonry is corrupt and ought to be abolished; but they are very cautious not to make an effort to accomplish this desirable end. They will whisper against masonry behind closed doors, but in public, the whole weight of their influence, in too many instances, goes to support its existence, and to weaken the hands and defeat efforts of those who labor to effect its overthrow.

I believe that those individuals in our congregations, who are masons, and claim to be Christians at the same time, and who say that they love the Lord with all their hearts, ought to renounce all connection with the institution, and absolve themselves from all allegiance to Masonic oaths.

My war is not with men, but with principles; not with masons, but with masonry; and my object is to see that institution destroyed, lock, stock and barrel; and not settle on something which will produce a temporary peace, and leave masonry standing, bidding defiance to "the world in arms," to put it down.

What good does it do for men to say, that they will have nothing more to do with masonry, and still hold themselves members of the institution, or bound by its oaths, to obey its laws, usages, and customs? This does not touch the evil. And this is the very thing that masonry wants. They are making every effort in their power to persuade churches to be satisfied with this compromise, and to go along with something which will leave masonry untouched as an evil.

Some may ask, "but if they will let masonry alone, forsake the lodges, and do nothing to support the institution, why will it not remove the evil?" I answer, because, it leaves them in full possession of the depraved principles of masonry, members of the institution, and masons as much as they ever were. For a man to pretend that he will have nothing to do with masonry in any of its forms, and will do nothing to support it, and yet will not renounce Masonic oaths, and declare them null and void, is a great absurdity; it is a plain contradiction. For he has sworn "to obey all signs and summonses given, handed, sent or thrown to him from the hand of a brother, or from the body of a legally constituted lodge."

Should he be summoned to attend a lodge meeting, a Masonic funeral, or any other Masonic parade, he must go; considers himself bound to go. Should he see a brother mason give the sign of distress, he must fly to his relief at the risk of his life, though that brother may be defending or supporting masonry. Should a master mason require him to go on his errand, and should that errand be to aid in a conspiracy to kidnap and murder; or to do anything else to defend or support masonry, he must go if he has to go barefoot and bareheaded. Should he be required to conceal the crimes of a brother mason, when called to testify against him, he must do it; and we may depend that he will do it, unless he will renounce the oath by which he is bound to do it. Now, where is his honesty in saying that he will do nothing directly, nor indirectly, to support masonry, yet will not renounce these oaths? Is there not reason to doubt his honesty? The fact is, he will support the lodge, or he will renounce his Masonic oath; and if he pretends to the contrary, to have nothing to do with masonry, and will not renounce these oaths, he is not to be depended on; for he is bound to obey the laws, usages and customs of the institution, and to support it to all intents and purposes. If he does not separate from it as an evil, and in a way which shall give people to understand that he believes it to be an evil, then the whole weight of his influence goes to support it. By a Masonic sign he may give the mystic brotherhood to understand, that he is a firm adherent of the order, and at the same time say to the church, "I have nothing to do with masonry." A man may just as well attend lodge meetings once a week, as to pretend to have nothing to do with masonry, yet cling to its obligations. He would act more like an honest man. Shall we hold men in good standing in the church of God, and even invest them with the office of the ministry, who will not renounce these oaths, in both word and deed?

Some people think that all a man has to do is take a dismission from the lodge and withdraw from it, and be under no obligation to the institution. But this is not true - It is not so easy for a man to free himself from the fangs of this monster, as we shall see from the following quotes: Carl Claudy 33°, in his book **Introduction To Freemasonry**, (p. 25) says - The candidate obligates himself for all time: "Once a mason, always a mason." He may take no interest in the Order. He may dimit, become unaffiliated, be dropped for Non Payment of Dues, be tried for a Masonic offense and suspended or expelled, but he cannot "unmake" himself as a Mason, or ever avoid the moral responsibility of keeping the obligations he **voluntarily** assumes. In the words of the Worshipful Master he is "bound to us by an obligation - a tie stronger than human hands can impose." Thomas Webb in **Webb's Monitor**, (p. 240) says - This covenant from the Masonic viewpoint is paramount to all others which a Mason may enter. It can never be repudiated nor laid aside. "We obligate them by solemn and irrevocable ties to perform the requirements of, and avoid the things prohibited by Masonry." "No law of the land can affect it, no anathema of the church can weaken it." The lodge may give him a demit and grant him the liberty of not attending lodge meetings except when summoned. Then he **must** attend. The oaths which he has taken are unconditional, and bind him to the institution in all causes, through life; and the only possible way he can be free of it, is to cast off the fetters and chains which these unhallowed oaths have placed upon him, and to turn his back on that cesspool of sin and blasphemy, as righteous Lot did on Sodom: and let him "remember Lot's wife." Every person who has impartially examined the subject, knows, that a greater abomination than masonry, never cursed the inhabitants of the earth. When men leave masonry, as Martin Luther left the Roman church, and as the heathen leaves his idols - then we can talk about their manifesting the spirit of the gospel.

Some people think that those individuals who renounce their Masonic oaths, degrade themselves, and render themselves unworthy of confidence. Nothing has surprised me more than to hear this kind of talk from professors of Christianity. To say that it is a disgrace for a man to renounce the blasphemous oaths administered in Masonic lodges, is like saying that it is a disgrace for the ignorant Hindoo to renounce his caste, and the worship of his gods. Shall he be disgraced for this noble deed, which is required by God, and over which the angels in heaven rejoice? Why then disgrace a man for renouncing masonry, which is more evil then that foul system of Hindoo idolatry? Those who renounce masonry are often attempted to be disgraced by the tongue of the malicious persecutor, as Luther and his companions were for renouncing popery, and violating their vows of celibacy. But their conduct is highly honorable in the eyes of God, and will be approved at the judgement seat of Christ.

I believe it is the duty of all truly born-again Christians, especially ministers of Christ and Sunday school teachers, who are masons, to publicly dissent from all connection with the Masonic lodge and to renounce it as wicked and ungodly. They have done wrong in the first place to join a secret society, a society which requires a savage oath, and a drawn sword to conceal itself from public scrutiny. They have done wrong, to swear, without any condition whatever, that they will do, they know not what. And they have done wrong in supporting the lodge up to this day. This wrong they ought to confess, and renounce, and bear public testimony against it. This the word of God requires, as we shall see from the following scripture: Leviticus 5:4-5 *"Or if a soul swear, pronouncing with his lips to do evil or to do good, whatsoever it be that a man pronounceth with an oath; and it be hid from him; when he knoweth of it, then he shall be guilty in one of these. And it shall be when he shall be guilty in one of these things, that he shall confess that he hath sinned in that thing."* This passage is right to the point. Masons swear to do something; but when they swear, the thing which they swear to do, is hid from them. They do not know whether it be good or evil; and no matter which it is; they have done wrong, and are bound to confess that they have sinned in pronouncing such an oath. To leave the practice of masonry without renouncing its principles as corrupt and wicked, is healing slightly the hurt of God's people; and there are men of sufficient discernment in almost every church to see this.

It is time that preachers spoke out against this evil and lay the axe at the root of the tree. Let the truth go forth under the power of God's Holy Spirit, and masonry couldn't find even a secret corner in the church of God, in which to hide its head.

BIBLIOGRAPHY

Blackmer, Rollin C. *The Lodge and The Craft.*
Macoy Publishing and Masonic Supply Co., Richmond, Va. 1976

Buck, J.D., *Symbolism of Mystic Masonry.*
Charles T. Powner Co., Chicago 1925

Cerza, Alphonse *Let There Be Light.*
The Masonic Service Ass., Silver Springs, Maryland 1987

Chase, Wingate G. *Digest of Masonic Law.* N/P

Claudy, Carl H. *Introduction to Freemasonry.*
The Temple Pub. Washington, D.C. 1985

Clymer, Dr. R. Swinburne, *The Mysticism of Masonry.*
Philosophical Publishing Co., California 1900

Coil, Henry W. *Coil's Masonic Encyclopedia.*
Macoy Publishing and Masonic Supply Co., New York, N.Y. 1961

Doesburg, Jacob O. *Freemasonry Illustrated.*
Ezra A. Cook Pub. Chicago 1892

Duncan, Malcolm *Duncan's Ritual.*
Charles T. Powner Co., Chicago 1974

Gould, James L. *Guide to the Royal Arch Chapter.*
Charles T. Powner Co., Chicago 1981

Haggard, Rev. Forrest D. *The Clergy and the Craft.*
Missouri Lodge of Research 1970

Hall, Manly P. *The Lost Keys of Freemasonry.*
Macoy Publishing and Masonic Supply Co., Richmond, Va. 1976

Haywood, H. L. *The Great Teachings of Masonry.*
George H. Doran Co. New York 1923

Hunt, George L. *Secret Societies.* N/P

Mackey, Albert G. Encyclopedia of Freemasonry.
The Masonic History Co., New York 1920

Mackey, Albert G. *Lexicon of Freemasonry.*
McClure Publishing Co., Philadelphia 1910

Mackey, Albert G. *Masonic Ritualist.* N/P

Mackey, Albert G. *Jurisprudence of Freemasonry.*
Ezra A. Cook, Chicago 1947

Mackey, Albert G. *Manual of the Lodge.*
Clark and Maynard Pub. Co., New York 1891

Mackey, Albert G. *Symbolism of Freemasonry.*
Charles T. Powner Co. Chicago 1975

Macoy, Robert *The True Masonic Guide.*
Clark, Austin & Smith Publishers, New York 1854

Macoy, Robert *The Masonic Manual.*
Clark & Maynard, New York 1853

Mc Cauley, L.M. *What About Masonry.* N/P

Mc Clain, Alva J. *Freemasonry and Christianity.* N/P

Moore, Cornelius *The Craftsman and Freemason's Guide.*
Jacob Ernst and Co., Cincinnati 1846

Newton, Rev. Joseph F. *The Men's House.*
Southern Publishers Inc., Kingsport, Tenn. 1923

Newton, Rev. Joseph F. *The Builders.*
George H. Doran Co., New York 1914

Pierson, A.T.C. *Traditions of Freemasonry.* N/P

Pike, Albert *Morals and Dogma.* Washington, D.C. 1963

Preuss, Arthur *A Study in American Freemasonry.*
B. Herder Book Co., St. Louis 1920

Richardson, Jabez, *Richardson's Monitor of Free-Masonry.*
David McKay Publisher, Philadelphia

Ronayne, Edmond *The Master's Carpet.*
Ezra A. Cook, Chicago 1982

Ronayne, Edmond *Chapter Degrees.*
Ezra A. Cook, Chicago 1984

Runquist, Felix *The Cross or The Compass.* N/P
—*Ritual of Freemasonry.*
W. Reeves Publisher, London

Shaw, Jim *The Deadly Deception.*
Huntington House, Lafayette, La. 1988

Sickels, Daniel *General Ahiman Rezon.*
The Masonic Publishing and Manufacturing Co., New York 1865

Sickels,Daniel *Mystic Masonry.* N/P

Steinmetz, George H. *Freemasonry-Its Hidden Meaning.*
Macoy Pub. and Masonic Supply Co., Richmond, Va. 1976

Storms, E.M. *Should a Christian be a Mason?*
New Puritan Library Inc., Fletcher, N.C. 1980
—*Standard Freemasonry Illustrated.*
Charles T. Powner Co. Chicago 1983
—*Scottish Rite Masonry* (2) Volumes.
Charles T. Powner Co. Chicago 1979

Ward, J.S.M. *Freemasonry: Its Aims & Ideals.*
William Rider & Son London 1923

Webb, Thomas Smith *The Freemasons Monitor.*
Published by Cushing and Appleton, Salem 1816

Whalen, William J. *Christianity and American Freemasonry.*
Our Sunday Visitor Publishing Div. Huntington, Indiana 1987

Wilmshurst, Walter L. *The Meaning of Masonry.*
Bell Publishing Co. New York 1980